D1202923

Welcome to the Big Time

Earnie Shavers

with Marshall Terrill

Foreword by Bert Randolph Sugar

Pulp Hero Press
The Most Dangerous Books on Earth
www.PulpHeroPress.com

Pulp Hero Press publishes its books in a variety of print and electronic formats. Some content that appears in one format may not appear in another.

Editor: Bob McLain
Layout: Artisanal Text

ISBN 978-1-68390-079-5
Printed in the United States of America

Pulp Hero Press | www.PulpHeroPress.com
Address queries to bob@pulpheropress.com

Contents

Foreword

The making of a great martini is much like the making of a great fighter.

In the case of the former, it is the correct mix of gin and vermouth at precisely the right moment, not a second too early nor too late; in the case of the latter, it is coming on the scene at precisely the right moment, not a second too early nor too late.

Unfortunately for Earnie Shavers, it was his fate to come along when the heavyweight division was crowded to overflowing with more aspirations, past, present, and future, than at any time in its long and storied history—with boxers like Ali, Frazier, Foreman, Norton, Holmes, Quarry, Lyle, Young, Chuvalo, Patterson, Ellis, Foster, Mathis, Bonavena, et cetera, etc., etc., all fighting for their place at the top of the heavyweight mountain.

And so today, when the name Earnie Shavers is mentioned, it is remembered by most as being part of the greatest class in the history of the heavyweight division more than being remembered for his own exploits, which were substantial.

More's the pity. For Earnie Shavers should be remembered as possessing the hardest punch in the history of the heavyweight division, a howitzer-like right so live it vibrated even while he slept. It was a right that landed with all the noise of a blast that fells six or seven bystanders and had opponents lining up on the side of the undertaker.

Twice Earnie came close enough to touch the hem of Dame Fortune's skirt—in his fights with Muhammad Ali and Larry Holmes. In both, he landed his haymaker on the chins of the respective worthies. But Ali faked him out, disguising his hurt and costing Earnie his chance at the championship; and Holmes, whose eyes were rotating in their parent sockets on his way down, was magically awakened when his head hit the canvas and came back to win.

And so Earnie's career has become defined by those losses—much as Billy Conn's was by his loss to Joe Louis and Jack Dempsey's by his loss to Gene Tunney. Which, as all things tend to be in the long run, is unfair.

To be fair you must examine the contents of the bottle, not just the bottle itself. And in the case of Earnie, it's his entire career that must be viewed, a career in which he won 73 fights, 67 by KO, for a slugging average of over .900—once scoring 27 knockouts in a row, to put him in the stratified realm of Joe DiMaggio for consecutive hits.

Even then you will not get the entire story of Earnie Shavers. For Earnie Shavers was more than just a helluva fighter. He also was—and still is—a helluva man. Allow me here to share a story with you, one which involved Earnie and yours truly.

The scene was a Boxing Writer's dinner back in the mid-90s. Among the guests assembled at the head table were Muhammad Ali and Earnie Shavers. Between the two, your willing story-teller. Somewhere between dinner courses, the guests decided that their dessert was to be Muhammad Ali's autograph and they descended upon the dais in one of the most riotous mob scenes since the days of the French Revolution. As the head table started to quake, I turned to Earnie and said something like, "Come on, let's get the hell out of here before we're run over."

However, Earnie held his ground and, his face swathed in good nature, merely said of the man with whom he had gone 15 rounds a few years before, "I want his autograph, too."

That, to me, was the quintessential Earnie Shavers: a man as soft-boiled outside the ring as he was hard-boiled in it, humble and as untaken with his feats as red wine blushing at the certificate of purity on its label.

So, when you remember the name Earnie Shavers, think not just of his prodigious power, nor of his many great fights. Think of the totality of this man. For Earnie Shavers serves as proof that time does not relinquish its hold over men or monuments. And in his case, he is both.

Bert Randolph Sugar
Boxing Historian
December 2001

CHAPTER ONE

Crazy in Alabama

The lights hanging over the ring exploded in my eyes. My entire world turned very weird. I reached for the ropes and tried to pull myself into an upright position. This was no way for my boxing career to end—against a journeyman fighter on foreign soil.

I was fighting on the undercard of Muhammad Ali's last hurrah, against Trevor Berbick on December 11, 1981, in Nassau, Bahamas. The whole event was a miserable operation. The show was held in a minor-league ballpark and started two hours late because no one could find a key to get into the place. The promoters had only two pairs of gloves for the whole event and they forgot to bring a bell. An old cow bell from someone's trunk was found at the last minute and used at ringside. Attendance was as dismal as the accommodations.

As if all that wasn't bad enough, there I was flat on my back against last-minute substitute Jeff Sims. I hadn't even planned to be on this card, but I had received a phone call shortly before the fight with an offer of $50,000 to fight my "grandma" (promoter slang for an opponent who should be a soft touch). It sounded like a decent payday with minimal risk. I agreed to the match and jetted down to the Bahamas 12 days before the fight date to help with press coverage.

I was thrown a whopping curve ball the minute I landed on the island. "Grandma" was out as my opponent and the replacement was fellow knockout artist Jeff Sims. The story I received was that my original opponent had taken ill, and since Sims was one of Ali's sparring partners, he was already in the Bahamas and was willing to take the match. I was at the twilight of my career, and a slugfest against this young tank wasn't my idea of an island vacation. So I decided on a preemptive strike.

At the weigh-in I approached Sims.

"Where's your trainer, Angelo Dundee?" I asked, acting like the man in charge.

Sims looked up at me, his annoyance obvious.

"I don't know," he said, clearly not wanting to get too chummy. But I really wasn't interested in being Sims' friend.

"You are just one of his niggers, he doesn't care about you at all," I told him, as nobody could care more about him than Uncle Earnie. "He's only interested in his cut of the purse."

"You're right man, he don't care," Sims readily agreed. If you want to push a black man's buttons, just talk about "the man" stealing a brother's money, and you have instant rapport. That night, prior to leaving our dressing room for the fight, I became Dear Abby again.

"Remember, don't get hurt tonight," I said to Sims in a protective manner, as if hurting him was the last thing on my own mind.

He responded with a puzzled look. I learned the power of psychology as an amateur boxer and was giving my opponent something to think about besides trying to knock me on my butt. As I got older, I learned to rely more on my brains than my brawn.

Sims only had 16 professional bouts, but his 12 victories had all come by knockout. Before the bout, I was told that he was a tremendous puncher. I was in semi-retirement and I feared for what this kid could do to me at my ripe old age. A black eye on my face was fine and would heal in due time. A black eye on my win/loss record I could ill afford on the downside of my career.

At the opening bell, Sims came out blazing. Seconds later, I was on the deck, courtesy of a Sims right hand. I was hurt and knew that I wasn't physically prepared for a 10-round war. After taking an eight-count, I grabbed Sims in a clinch.

"Slow down, Jeff, we got 10 rounds to go," I said, appealing to his sense of fairness. "Put it in low gear, brother."

Sims nodded in agreement. When the bell sounded to end the round, my head was still spinning.

By the second round, the cobwebs had cleared, and I was back in the fight. Being the perfect gentleman, Sims eased his pace. By the fourth round, I was in control of the bout.

Then I found my opening.

I drilled Sims with my patented right hand and sent him down for the 10 count.

After the contest, Sims approached me with the look of a kid who'd just gotten mugged by his favorite uncle.

"Mr. Shavers, you lied to me about 10 rounds," he said in a hurt tone. Well, he was still calling me "mister." He could have called me a whole lot worse after the stunt I pulled on him.

I couldn't hold back my smile and I threw my arms wide open.

"Jeff, welcome to the Big Time!"

For someone who had once seemed destined for a life in the cotton fields, I had reached the big time in boxing and in life. I've had a tremendous life, but I've also had my share of hard times. I've knocked out former world champions Jimmy Ellis and Ken Norton and given champions Muhammad Ali and Larry Holmes some of their toughest battles. But if it had not been for an unwelcome visit by the Ku Klux Klan, I might never have left the Deep South and climbed into a boxing ring and been able to achieve my dreams.

I can still remember when I was a little boy sitting and listening to my mother tell us stories about the Deep South. She would talk about how hard life was during her childhood. Life had always been difficult for African Americans in the South, and that included everyone before me on the Shaver family tree. That's not a misprint by the way—I was born Earnie Dee Shaver on August 31, 1944, in Garland, Alabama, a small town 50 miles north of Mobile. The "s" came later in life after I developed my famed knockout punch.

All 10 of us Shaver children would spend hour after hour working with our mother, who was the true leader in our household. I was the fifth child born to Willie Belle and Curtis Shaver. I had three older brothers, LeRoy, Johnny, and Luther, and an older sister, Rubie. Younger than me were brothers Theo and Alvin, and sisters Grace, Gloria, and Delores. We were a close family that worked together and slept together. All six Shaver boys bunked in the same room. If one of my brothers coughed or snored all night, nobody slept unless it was on account of a knockout punch delivered by one of us. But at the time, I didn't know there was any other way of life. Blacks all over the Deep South faced similar struggles, and our story was one of perseverance through grit and wit.

As early as the age of five, I remember picking cotton. I suppose it was hard work, but I knew no other lifestyle. Long days in the field were the norm for all of us. We were poor, with no phone, electricity, or indoor plumbing. We had an outhouse and drank from a well. The best hope for a black growing up in the South was to just survive. I remember when my brother Johnny got bitten by a rattlesnake and almost died before my very eyes. Life was a day-to-day struggle.

All Momma ever did was work, even when she was a child herself. When the subject of work came up, Dad made himself scarce. Over the course of time, we all became closely attached to our mother because of her quiet, steadfast example. She was always there for us, and so a strong bond of love that lasted a lifetime was formed. My mother was a wonderful God-fearing lady who instilled in each of us kids at a very early age the idea that through prayer and faith in God, all things are possible. That was how we survived—through our mother's prayers and her faith in God. Our mother taught us to love everyone, and that even included the Ku Klux Klan members who would raid our home in Alabama.

Our mother had little in the way of a formal education, but she had so much common sense and what I call "God smarts." She was so well-versed in the Bible that it compensated for her lack of schooling. The lessons she taught us growing up helped us make sound decisions for the rest our of lives. But more important than her lessons were the examples she set for us.

Looking back, I remember the feeling of hopelessness we had in the South. There were no opportunities for advancement for blacks at all, unless it was advancement to the great beyond. If you were white and poor, at least there were a few doors open to you. If you were black, all you hit were roadblocks.

I remember the long walks to our segregated small school-house. Our family couldn't even afford paper lunch bags. We wrapped our lunch in old newspapers white people discarded. The teachers in the South didn't care if we learned or not.

They were living in the same hopeless environment, and hope was a dangerous thing if there was nothing to back it up. If a student was absent from class, the teachers didn't seem to mind much. It was one less kid for them to baby-sit. Blacks weren't expected to graduate in the Deep South, anyway. By the time most kids were 10, they had graduated to a lifetime of work in the fields. But a surprise visit by the Ku Klux Klan changed my life forever.

I still get the chills thinking about the incident that spurred the Shaver family to take refuge and flee north to Ohio. When I was five, my father bought a mule from a local white man. Dad had agreed to make the payments for the mule in installments, and every payment was made on time until he had just two of them left. Then came a bad harvest in 1950. The combination of the hot Alabama sun burning bright down on the red dirt and the boll weevils that ate up all the cotton that year caused one of the worst crops in years.

The white man's patience had run thin and he drove up to our house hurling racial epithets at my father.

"Nigger, you better pay me the rest of my money!" he raged on our own front porch. "I want it all now, or I will take that mule away with me."

My father pleaded for an extension, saying he needed just a little more time to work his fields.

Even though the white man knew it was a bad year for harvest, he wouldn't make any compromises, especially with a black man. He didn't need to, because the law was on his side. He marched right into our barn and got the mule. In desperation, my father fetched his rifle from the house. When he came back out, the white man was leading the mule out of the barnyard gate.

My father cocked back the hammer of the gun and pointed it at him.

"Turn the mule loose, or else," Dad commanded. The man stared hard at my father and released the mule. The battle had been won, but war had now been declared. As the man left our property, he had some parting words for my father.

"Nigger, I'll be back tonight," he promised with a gleam in his eye. My dad had committed the ultimate unforgivable sin in the Deep South: he defied the white man. And a member of the Ku Klux Klan, at that. Back then, the Klan took no quarter.

It was an era of great racial divide in America. Black folks were not supposed to look white people in the eye when they talked to them, and they certainly did not pull a gun on them. Negroes, as they were commonly called, were supposed to know their place, and my father, even though he was protecting his own home and property, had crossed the line.

Knowing this, my mother sent my brother LeRoy to get my grandfather, who lived about a quarter of a mile away. When Grandpa, Bud Shaver, arrived, my mother told him what happened with the Klansman.

Bud Shaver had spent his entire life in Alabama, and instinctively knew what was going to happen. There was going to be a good old-fashioned lynching for this. He had not only heard about lynchings by the Ku Klux Klan, but had seen a few of his friends meet their maker, and for pettier infractions than the one my father had committed. He wasn't about to see his own son hanging lifelessly at the end of a rope because of a momentary lapse of reason.

"You must go up north to my brother's home in Ohio," Bud warned my father. "If you stay here, the Klan will surely kill you."

He didn't mean tomorrow, either. Leaving time was right now. Bud hitched up the mule and wagon and immediately took my father to the train station in Georgiana, a town about five miles from Garland.

Dad purchased a ticket on the next train headed to Ohio, never to return to the South.

Later that evening, as Grandpa predicted, we were visited by 20 Klansmen, all dressed in the traditional white hoods and carrying burning torches. It wasn't a social call. They came with the intent to kill my father, but he was nowhere to be found. I still remember how frightened I felt as the madmen burst through the front door of our home. My heart was in my throat.

They ransacked the house, a typical three-room shotgun shack, for what seemed like an eternity. I remember them shouting and yelling racial epithets while my body shook with fear.

"Come on out, nigger! We want to show you what we do to niggers who pull a gun on a white man in the South," taunted one of them. Eventually they left, but they vowed to get their revenge one day.

That was it—my father could never come back home. The Klan would make random checks from time to time to see if my father had come back. After a few months, they finally stopped, believing they'd scared him off for good. The odd thing is, as frightening as the Klan was, they also had a weird sense of honor. They never harmed any of us children or my mother. It was Dad's black hide they wanted.

My father settled in with my great-uncle in Newton Falls, Ohio. He found a good-paying factory job at Rockwell Standard, making car bumpers. He sent money to my mother every week to help out. Mama did the best she could to feed ten hungry kids by herself, and Dad saved enough money in six months to send for the rest of the family.

My mother packed all of our possessions, which wasn't much, and all the neighbors lent a hand getting us ready for our move. We packed boxes of food for the long journey, because buying food on the train was beyond our small budget. Our generous neighbors made sure we had plenty to eat and drink. It was a time in our society when people cared about their neighbors.

We left Alabama in December 1950. It was cold out and snow flurries were falling. The weather was very unusual for Alabama as it rarely snowed there. It was the very first time I had seen snow in the South. I thought it was so beautiful that I forgot for a few minutes how really crazy it was in Alabama.

CHAPTER TWO

Back to Ohio

Many black families moved up North during this time in search of a better life. For the Shaver family, it was no different.

The long train ride was a new experience for me. The train winded and twisted through the northern part of Alabama and then passed through the mountainous terrain of Tennessee and through the blue-green grass of Kentucky, and finally stopped at our destination: northern Ohio.

During the long journey, Mom made the North sound full of promise. I remember sitting in the "colored section" of the train gazing out the window at all the different landscapes. I was only a little kid and had no idea what this strange land called "the North" would hold for me. I could only dream about what lay ahead, and instinctively knew that anything was better than Alabama. It turned out to be the best thing that ever happened to me.

We were leaving behind the hard times most black share-croppers lived through. For example, in Alabama I probably hadn't traveled any farther than 500 yards away from my parents' home. A black family in the South could never hope to do much better than pick cotton. The new start up North gave us hope.

After the long journey, we were ready to begin our new lives. The train whistle sounded as we pulled into our station in Newton Falls, Ohio, a city with a population of about 4,000 people. I remember it so well because the ground was covered with about six inches of snow. Our family—including our father, who was waiting at the station—piled into two cabs. The cab ride was only two miles out to my father's uncle's house in the small farming community of Braceville, outside of Newton Falls.

There were so many uncles, aunts, and cousins waiting at the house to welcome us. Everyone was so nice to us, and I knew that our new home was going to be great.

We shared the place with my father's Uncle Dan and Aunt Lola Shaver. All of their children had moved out, but they were raising a grandson, Billy. Our family had the upstairs portion of the home, three bedrooms. Things were pretty crowded, but we somehow managed to stay out of each other's way and live in harmony.

Five of us were school-aged, and we enrolled at Newton Falls Elementary School. There was a big difference in the schools in the North in that they were a more advanced public school system, but we mostly adjusted. My older brothers had more difficulty than I did. They were behind scholastically compared to their counterparts in the North. I was young enough that it didn't seem to affect me as much. I enjoyed academics and was a quick learner.

We took a bus to school, which was a real luxury to us. We made new friends, even with the white kids. The school contained about 10 percent minorities, but it really didn't matter. White people in the North treated my family with respect, something that took some getting used to. Even though we were poor and spoke with a Southern accent, I made a lot of friends in a short time.

The teachers' attitudes were also different than in the South. They were actually concerned with my academic progress as opposed to having the attitude of, "Well, you'll never be anything but a sharecropper, anyway." I'll never forget my first grade teacher, Mrs. Sloan. She held me to a higher standard in the classroom and helped with my homework. She also scolded me if my schoolwork was unsatisfactory. I excelled in mathematics and history. Our way of life was so much better in such a short time.

Another difference in the North was that the whole community helped raise everyone's kids. The concept of "it takes a village to raise a child" was one we understood long before Hillary Clinton popularized it. If you were a child and got caught doing something wrong, it was an unwritten rule that the adult who caught you was allowed to give you a spanking if they thought you needed it. And you prayed to God that they didn't tell your parents, because another ass whipping would be in the cards when you got home. My brothers and sisters and I knew better than to be a problem to anyone because our mother meant business when it came to raising her children right. She did not play around when it came to disciplining us. If we got out of hand, Lord have mercy!

When we got home from school we did our designated chores and then our homework. Aunt Lola would prepare dinner for her family first and serve them a hearty meal. After they finished, my mother would prepare our meal. The facilities weren't big enough for both of them to use at the same time.

We lived that way for about a year until my father, with some help from relatives, built us our own home on farmland in Braceville. We had a five-acre plot of land next to the woods for which my father must have paid no more than $2,000. My father, with the help of his friends, Frank Bremer and Henry Brook, took about a year to build a two-story home out of wood and cinder blocks. I grew to love our farm's location because it was secluded and near the woods.

We raised livestock: goats, sheep, chickens, pigs, and a few cows. We churned our own butter and grew beans, tomatoes, corn, and wheat. It was back-breaking work, but rewarding when it came time to eat. I remember waking up early to milk the cows and watching Dad plow into the darkness. These disciplined work habits carried over into everything I did as an adult and helped me realize early that success is 90 percent perspiration. Although my family was poor, we were self-sufficient and proud. All the food I ate, we raised. I never gave hard work a second thought. It was a way of life.

During my free time, I spent many happy hours exploring every inch of the woods, taking long walks and dreaming about what I wanted to be in life. Mostly, I dreamed about becoming a great athlete. I knew athletes made good money. Although I wasn't crazy about sports, I figured that excelling in sports would be a way to help my family out of our financial difficulties.

When I wasn't dreaming about becoming a pro athlete, I fancied myself as a young Davy Crockett. I hunted, fished, camped, and trapped muskrats and weasels. I loved that small farm in Braceville and the sense of freedom it gave me.

Besides lending a hand on our farm, I also worked as a hired hand in the neighbors' fields, harvesting corn, threshing wheat, or cutting hay. In the fall I would chop down trees for firewood. I would also earn my Christmas money by selling the furs of muskrats. I had seen an ad in *Field and Stream* magazine mentioning where I could send the hides to New York and get $2.25 a skin. The $100 or so I made that way always went to Mom for Christmas presents.

My brothers also worked neighboring farms for extra money to contribute to the family income, and my sisters sold strawberries at a roadside stand. We never had a lot of extras growing up, but there was always plenty to eat and we got by.

Working on the farm was good for me. It gave me the motivation to become successful. I knew that I didn't want to work the fields for the rest of my life. Little did I know then that the heavy work I was required to do on the farm was making my body strong and developing it for my life's work—boxing.

At the time, I was unaware the strenuous farm life would be such a great asset later on. Growing up on the farm was one of the best things that ever happened to me. After I turned 12, my parents never had to buy me another thing. I earned enough to buy my own clothes and school supplies.

My older brother LeRoy was friends with a talented local high-school football star named Sonny Griffin, who soon became a mentor to me. Griffin was a standout on the gridiron, and I took an instant liking to him. When he came by the house I would ask what it took to be a successful athlete. Griffin told me what I had to do to prepare myself to be good. He told me that I had to live clean, no smoking or drinking liquor, and that I had to maintain a healthy diet.

Looking back, everything I have done in life in one form or another helped me prepare for becoming an athlete. At that young age, I still had no idea what my chosen field in sports would be, but I knew that I wanted a decent life and that doing hard labor for minimum wage was not the answer for me.

Another advantage of growing up in the country and working on a farm was that there was little chance of getting into trouble. Most of my time was taken up with work or helping out the neighbors. When I wasn't working, I spent time in the woods. By most people's standards, I guess it was a very boring life. But not to me, because the outdoors fascinated me and held my interest. I enjoyed that kind of lifestyle. I suppose you could say it made me a square—I didn't take drugs, I didn't drink alcohol, and I didn't smoke marijuana.

By the time I enrolled in Newton Falls High School, my excellent physical condition allowed me to become a record-breaking athlete for the Newton Falls Tigers.

All of my hard work paid off when I tried out for the freshman football team. Practice was tough, but I thoroughly enjoyed it. We usually started in the beginning of August, a few weeks before school opened. We practiced twice a day in the blistering humid Ohio heat. During the season, attending football practice meant missing the bus home after school. But I never minded the long walk home.

The hard training actually didn't affect me much because physically I was way ahead of everyone else. I enjoyed the competitiveness of sports, and I won the position of starting left halfback on the junior varsity. I also was a natural fullback.

I enjoyed playing football my freshman year, and the varsity coach, Andy Pike, encouraged me to work hard in the offseason. He thought I had the talent and potential to help the varsity squad as a sophomore. But something happened that changed everything. At that point in my life, I was still a follower and didn't think for myself, which led to a decision that I regret to this day.

A few other minority students felt they were being mistreated on the football field. They argued that they were not getting playing time because of their race, first and foremost. I instantly sided with my fellow African Americans, and boycotted my next two years of football with them. While they sat around bitching, I began to see that these guys weren't really protesting racial injustice; they just wanted something to protest. I was a fool for not taking stock of the situation and coming to my own conclusion, and I suffered as a result.

I came to my senses my senior year and rejoined the team, and was a contributing factor in our winning squad. I moved to the left end position, playing both offense and defense. Who knows? If I had bothered to think for myself two years earlier, I might have become a standout at the college level. As it turned out, I never could make up for those lost years, and my fellow boycotters mostly turned out to be bums. Quitting the football team set the tone for the rest of their lives. At least it didn't become a pattern in my life.

Meanwhile, my mother worked as a maid at two local motels. Every day she changed beds and cleaned up the mess most people left behind when they checked out. During the football season I also worked at a local motel, making 75 cents an hour cleaning rooms and picking weeds. This is why later on when I became a world traveler I always made sure to leave a tip for the maid every day I stayed in a hotel room. It's probably one of the most thankless and hardest occupations someone can do.

My mother was the hardest-working person I ever knew. Throughout my time in high school, she was the main source of income for our family. Dad had lost his job at the factory and decided it was time to retire. Although he had no savings and we were still poor, Dad was essentially just too lazy to work. He mostly sat around all day, smoking cigarettes and drinking coffee. While my mom was busting her hump with a variety of steady jobs, Dad was content to be a man of leisure when he couldn't afford to be.

My mother also did house cleaning for some white people in the nearby town of Warren. Eventually she took a decent-paying job at Warren General Hospital. Mom was an amazing woman of great strength and integrity. She supplemented our income by growing extra crops on the family farm. She sold the tastiest strawberries, watermelons, and all sorts of vegetables that never made it to our dinner table. She had a green thumb when it came to produce, and it rubbed off on her kids. Mom taught us her secret of picking the produce when it was ready.

My industrious mom was also a small-time entrepreneur who sold hair products to the black community, something else that rubbed off on me.

Word got around Warren that my mother was a hard worker. Ms. Tortorete, a prominent woman in the Warren community, hired Mom to work at the Christ Episcopal Church. My mother loved that job so much, and eventually my brothers and I also worked at the church in several capacities and reaped some fulfilling fringe benefits. We set up for all the banquets, parties, and dances. As soon as a banquet finished, my siblings and I enjoyed a feast of the leftover meals. I used to stuff myself full of the tastiest delicacies known to man. After putting in a long night of labor, the end-of-the-evening smorgasbord made it all worthwhile.

During the summer and fall months, we also worked every weekend cutting the grass at the church. In the wintertime we would shovel snow from the driveways and walking paths. I was such a hard worker I didn't have time to get into trouble. Which is just as well, since I daydreamed about being a gangster. For some reason I was infatuated with mobsters (Warren had its share of people in organized crime), and this continuing fascination would one day lead me to the wrong people.

While I fantasized about becoming a professional hitman, I was a choirboy—literally. I met my future wife, La Verne Payne, during a Thursday night choir practice at our church. She was a few years younger than me and attended nearby Braceville High. La Verne had a reputation as an excellent student and was also a standout in track and field. She also was known as a woman who diligently guarded her virginity. Nobody ever scored on La Verne. She was beautiful and intriguing to me, and her virginity presented a real challenge. One night at choir practice, I smiled at La Verne and offered her a piece of Juicy Fruit gum, which I always kept handy. Eventually, I asked her out.

On our first date we went to the annual donkey basketball game. It wasn't as romantic as it sounds, nor as easy. First I had to get past her father, Clifford Payne.

The Payne family had a respected name in the area, and Mr. Payne was very protective of his daughter. The FBI doesn't screen potential G-men as diligently as he screened La Verne's dates. The first night I went to pick up La Verne for a date, Mr. Payne kept me out on the front porch for well over an hour.

It occurred to me that nobody made it with La Verne because they couldn't get past Mr. Payne. I made sure that La Verne returned home well before curfew that night.

Surprisingly, Mr. Payne took a liking to me.

"La Verne, this is a hard-working young man," Mr. Payne smiled at her. It was his subtle way of saying he definitely approved of me. It was a reaction she hadn't seen from her father before where her beaus were concerned. But years later La Verne confided to me that she thought she would never see me again after the sermon her father had laid on me out on that porch.

La Verne and I began dating my senior year. When I wasn't working or training for the track team, I was with her.

In the spring of 1963, I broke the school record for the 440-yard dash with a time of 50.3. It was quite a feeling breaking the record, but there were no professional opportunities that I was aware of for a track star. And thanks to my ill-conceived boycott, I had blown any chance at a big-time football scholarship. A few small schools sent feelers my way about a partial scholarship, but I didn't have the resources to fund the rest of my education. I became frustrated and hoped I wasn't destined for a life in a factory. I still had big dreams of becoming an athlete. I just wasn't sure about the sport. Boxing wasn't even om my radar screen yet.

My senior year of high school, I was voted "Most Friendly Male." Strangely enough, I am pictured in my yearbook with a pair of boxing gloves in a mock duke-out with "Most Friendly Female," Evelyn Wright. But it would still be four more years until I laced on boxing gloves for more than show.

CHAPTER THREE

Betwixt and Between

After graduation, I took a job with B & O Railroad as a track man. It was a dirty, low-paying job. I came home filthy every night from hefting railroad ties all day long. I knew right away I didn't want to do that for the rest of my life. I worked at B & O Railroad for three weeks and despised every single miserable minute of it. It was time to make tracks for a new profession.

After I turned in my notice at B & O, I started work at Poison Rubber Factory in Garrettsville, Ohio, about 35 miles away. I made inner tubes for car and truck tires. Both the work and the pay were a vast improvement over the previous job. I worked with good people and developed some nice friendships. Because I had been raised that way by my mother, I always gave a little bit more than was expected of me and I moved up the ladder quickly to better jobs at the factory. In no time, I became a utility man with an increase in pay. Life seemed good on the outside, but I still felt unfulfilled inside. Surely this wasn't all there was to life?

Then some more responsibility came into my life—La Verne was pregnant, and she wanted me to talk to her father about our future. It was a talk I wasn't looking forward to.

I'll never forget the day that I went to speak to Mr. Payne about marrying his daughter. He had grown fond of me over the course of our courtship, but I was uptight about asking him for permission to marry La Verne. As soon as I brought up the subject of marriage to Mr. Payne, I sensed he knew there was more to the story. He responded in his typically intimidating voice, "You want to marry my daughter? Or you have to marry my daughter?" I remember fumbling out a few incoherent words before Mr. Payne extended his hand to congratulate me and welcome me to the family.

La Verne and I were married in a small ceremony in the town hall in Braceville. We rented a small house for $100 a month at 1054 Wood Street in Warren.

Our first child, Tamara Lynn, was born on April 18, 1965. I continued to work at Poison's, but the 45-minute commute each way was taking its toll on me. I put in every minute of overtime offered so I could sock away a few extra dollars, but I rarely saw my family or friends. La Verne and I decided I should look for a job closer to home.

Before I knew it, another daughter, Cyndi La Verne, was born on July 16, 1966. While I was happy with my growing family, my dreams of leaving the factory were slowly slipping away.

Fortunately, I found a job at Ideal Foundry in Newton Falls, which was seven miles from my home in Warren. I spent my days heating up large furnaces used to melt steel. It was extremely hot work, of course, and some days I would sweat off at least 10 pounds. I put in my share of overtime at this job, too.

In my limited spare time, I hung around with my buddies instead of staying at home with La Verne and the kids. I blew off a lot of steam by racing fast cars and got involved in drag racing on the streets. I enjoyed the adrenaline rush of speed, but after nearly losing my life in an accident, I decided to stay away from drag racing. I had a Chevelle painted up like the USA 1, but it read USA 2. I took off one night racing on Route 422, and lost control of the vehicle and went over an embankment. I should have been killed. After that, I took the car apart and never raced again. I craved excitement and soon found it in other ways.

I began spending more time with my cousin, Big George Horne, and his friend, Allan Scott. I had known both men for some time, George since high school and Allan from my drag-racing days. One day we were discussing why I changed jobs, and during our discussion, one topic led to another. Big George was the town thug and always carried a .44 magnum. His illegal activities brought a new level of excitement into my life, and fed my continuing daydreams about gangsterism.

Big George was into some bad stuff, too. In fact, he was a hit man for the Mafia, a stone-cold killer. As Elvis Presley once sang, if I was looking for trouble, I came to the right place. I didn't need to look any further than George.

Whenever I returned home from an all-nighter with Big George, I learned that La Verne had stayed up all night praying for my safety. Out of sheer desperation and panic, she would even call my mother and they would pray together. La Verne feared for my life because she knew everything Big George touched got tainted. Thinking back on those days, I realize there were times I really put La Verne through hell as I tried to figure out my path in life.

Although Big George was a professional hoodlum, I enjoyed his company. He had a certain charisma about him that was different than most men, and he had the confidence to do whatever he pleased without fearing the repercussions. I steered clear of the major felonies he trafficked in and certainly was never witness to any of his many "hits"; but if he needed help collecting some unpaid debt, I was always willing to lend a fist or two.

Most of the time, however, I used the power of intimidation to collect the cash. I knew that I was already an imposing figure. "If you don't pay the money, it will be the last time you ever see your family," I'd say, raising my voice and slamming my fist on the table. That usually did the trick. My collection rate was better than most telemarketers today, at about 99.9 percent. One time I scared a dope dealer so badly he went to the FBI for protection and I backed off and gladly gave up my perfect collection rate. I didn't think I could intimidate those boys.

Since my lemming-like behavior as a freshman gridiron star, I had learned to become a leader and make my own choices. Everything I have ever done, good or bad, was because that's what I wanted to do at that point in my life. Some guys I knew were getting $2,500 to $5,000 a hit—good money in those days. There was money to be made in the killing game.

Did the life of a killer appear glamorous? I can't say that it did. Exciting, perhaps, but not glamorous. Most of the people who were getting knocked off were dope dealers who got high on their own junk or degenerate gamblers who took out a loan with an unusually high amount of interest and got behind in their payments. Let's just say they took their habits to a whole new level once Big George or one of his colleagues got a hold of them.

I became so good at sizing up a situation that it got to the point where I could recognize a killer's style. One guy I knew liked to kill people by shooting them in the back of the head with a .22. Another guy would put them in the trunk of their own car and set it on fire. Another would have the person hog-tied and put a bullet through his temple. When I look back, it's scary that I befriended these guys.

Before I started boxing, I hung out with criminals because I liked them. Even to this day, I must admit—I still like them. There is something about the Mafia lifestyle that has always excited and intrigued me. It is so different from the life of a working-class man. Perhaps it was the idea that they did whatever they wanted to do. They didn't punch a time clock, they were the boss for the most part. They got the best seats in the house, they had the prettiest girls on their arms, they dressed nicely and were respected wherever they went.

One time, I almost crossed the line. My younger brother Alvin was killed by his ex-wife's boyfriend for insurance money. He was killed by a man named Lee Harvey.

Alvin and his wife had not been living with each other for quite some time when she came to my brother and asked if they could give it another go. Alvin said yes and took her back. His wife said that she had to get her clothes at Harvey's place, who would not let her have them. My brother promised to go with her to retrieve them.

Right before they got to Harvey's apartment, she gave my brother a gun to carry "just in case." The gun was empty, and my brother did not bother to check the chamber. When they got to Harvey's apartment, Harvey pulled a gun on Alvin and shot him. Because my brother had a gun in his possession and was in Lee Harvey's apartment, Lee was cleared of murder and got off on self-defense.

My brother's ex-wife got the insurance money with no problem and left town.

Because I had friends on both sides of the law, I knew step by step what had gone down. After I gathered the information, I had several people offer to kill both Lee Harvey and my brother's ex-wife. But this was personal. If they were going to die, it was going to be from my own two hands.

I had planned the perfect murder for two years as I watched the triggerman's every move. I knew how I was going to do it, where I was going to do it, how I was going to dispose of his body, and what airtight alibi I'd use.

You see, Lee Harvey was a Black Panther, a radical black militant group, and wasn't so well loved by the law. If a Black Panther met his maker, you could count on the law not to spend much time finding his killer. I even consulted an attorney friend of mine before I made my final decision. His advice even threw me for a loop.

"Earnie, if you are going to kill Lee Harvey, make sure that you are not in his apartment when it happens," the attorney advised me. He added that if my gun was still not smoking when the policemen came, he could easily get me off on account of Harvey being a Black Panther.

I contemplated killing Harvey several times, but each time I neared the point of no return, God spoke to me.

"Vengeance is mine," I heard an inner voice tell me. I pulled back and decided that Lee Harvey and Alvin's ex-wife must face God on Judgment Day and account for themselves. It was not for me to take it upon myself to play God. Ultimately, I credit God for not allowing me to enter into that lifestyle. He seemed to pull me back every time things got too dangerous or too close for comfort. I guess it was that old Mafia adage of "either you take care of the business, or the business will take care of you" that kept me on the straight and narrow.

For the record, let's just say since my last association with those guys, I've conveniently developed amnesia regarding names, dates, and places. A real bad case of amnesia. So bad, I'm certain I'll never be able to remember again.

Years later Big George would be gunned down in a paid hit-for-hire. He had fooled around with the wrong guy's wife—a big no-no in the Mafia book of unwritten rules.

Big George knew it was a dangerous lifestyle, and it ultimately was his downfall. I saw too many guys I knew get killed or end up in prison, and I scaled back my gangster affiliations drastically.

After working at Ideal Foundry for a year and a half, I was hired at General Motors in Lordstown, Ohio, which had only been open for a couple of months. It was just two miles from my home.

They offered great benefits, better pay, and I could make a better living for my family. But the assembly line work could be tedious. I used to daydream, wondering to myself how I could get out of that place outside of robbing a bank.

I put in overtime every day I could, but the amount varied from day to day. Most days it would be 45 minutes, but some days it was longer. I couldn't plan any activities in my life because I never knew if I would be called in to work overtime or how much extra time I needed to put in on any given day. Even though I had a wonderful wife, two great kids, and a good paying job, inside I was still empty and it pained me. I had a need in my life, a certain something I had to fulfill. I knew I was destined to be somebody. What it was, I didn't know, but the feeling was still there, churning away in the pit of my stomach.

After years of constant dreaming, I still had a burning desire in my gut to become a professional athlete—and time was running out for this married father of two.

An area boxer and close friend, Richard Austin, a former welterweight Golden Gloves champion, invited me to visit his boxing gym. I had become friendly with Austin back in my drag-racing days. Austin ran with a tough crowd, but he would never introduce me to any of them. I later discovered he was one of the biggest drug dealers in the area. Notwithstanding Austin's line of work outside the ring, he knew boxing and felt that with my strength and athletic ability I would be a natural for the ring. I declined Austin's initial offers to visit the gym, but eventually I took him up on it. The date still sticks in my head, and on January 3, 1967, I discovered my future occupation.

I can remember everything like it happened yesterday. Austin and I made the 15-mile drive to Youngstown and pulled up in front of the West Federal Street YMCA. Richard told me that I would like his amateur coach, Pedro Tomez. According to him, Pedro was one of the finest amateur coaches in the country.

Upon our entrance in the gym, Pedro Tomez noticed us and immediately made his way over. Austin had tipped him off about this new heavyweight prospect.

"How much do you weigh, young man?" Tomez asked.

"About 220 pounds."

"Have you ever boxed before?"

"No."

"With a build like that you can become heavyweight champion of the world and make yourself lots of money," he said.

The man certainly got my attention. Pedro asked if I wanted to give it a try, and I said yes. He put me in the ring with John Henry, who had won the area Golden Gloves title the previous year. Henry out-boxed me and frustrated me with his fluid movement and crisp jabs. I felt out of my element. But then I caught him with a right hand and he flew across the ring. Suddenly, the ring didn't feel quite so foreign.

In the background, I could hear Tomez rave about my one-punch power to my friend. Pedro was in Austin's face, "Did you see that?" Tomez's positive reaction meant a lot to me.

On the trip to Youngstown, Austin had filled me in on Pedro's impressive coaching credentials. Tomez's amateur boxing club had won over 10 team titles in Golden Gloves competition, and Pedro had just been named coach of the U.S. amateur boxing team which would be fighting in the Pan-American Games in Columbia, South America.

After the first round of the sparring session ended, I felt winded. Pedro instructed me to relax. He explained that I was too tense in the ring and was burning myself out.

I tried to follow directions, but I just couldn't. Again in the second round, Henry gave me a boxing lesson. Just as he was putting the final touches on my facial leather massage, I caught him with another right hand on the chin and sent him falling back into the ropes, but at the same time, I almost fell over from exhaustion.

At the conclusion of that first sparring session, Pedro shouted, "Man, have I got me a heavyweight here! If you dedicate yourself, you will be champ someday, kid. You've already got the punch!"

John Henry seconded the motion.

"Pedro, this guy can really punch, he is going to hurt somebody," Henry said.

Although winded from my six minutes sparring, I felt excited and enthused about boxing. Pedro asked when I would be back in the gym. I wanted to tell him I would be back the next day, but I was taking up the sport as an adult with a plate already full of responsibilities. With two daughters at home and a full-time factory job, I gave Pedro an honest reply.

"Let me go home and talk it over with my wife, and think about it for a week," I said, even as I knew deep down inside this was the future I wanted.

I could see disappointment in Pedro's eyes as he spoke. He had seen my potential in the ring, and didn't want my obvious talents to go to waste.

"Don't wait too long, because the Golden Gloves is in two weeks," Tomez said.

Upon arriving home that evening, I told La Verne what had happened at the gym and mentioned my desire to become a boxer. She did not share Pedro Tomez's excitement over that idea.

"Oh, no, Earnie Shaver. What if you get hurt, who's going to pay the bills?" I was the family breadwinner; La Verne's full-time job was as head of the household.

But I wasn't going down without a fight.

"Don't worry about me, I can take care of myself. Nobody is going to hurt me," I pleaded.

"No, Earnie, that's it! I don't want to talk about it," she said, laying down the law.

Although I was taking in a decent wage at General Motors, I felt that emptiness inside. In my heart the dream of becoming a professional athlete was still alive. I kept thinking of my first day in the boxing gym and how I trounced my first opponent. The words of encouragement from boxing guru Pedro Tomez replayed over and over in my mind. That, and the prospective fortune he spoke of, made my mouth water. I knew at the age of 22 I was a latecomer to the sport, but if Pedro believed in me, I knew I had to give it my best shot. This was probably my last opportunity to give any sport a last chance. The Cleveland Browns sure as hell weren't calling.

After returning from work the next day, I brought up the subject again with La Verne. I told her that she was married to the future heavyweight champion of the world. This time she smiled before lowering the boom.

"Sure thing, Earnie, now take out the trash, champ!" She thought this was just a phase I was going through to get out of the rut of factory life. But when I finally convinced her I was serious, she gave in. La Verne was always a supportive wife, even if my ambitions seemed far-fetched at the time.

I drove back to the gym in Youngstown to begin training for the approaching Golden Gloves competition. Pedro saw me and his face lit up. I told him that I was ready to box, and he proclaimed, "I got me a heavyweight champion."

I had only one week to train before the tournament started. Pedro sat me down and told me what I had to do if I wanted to make it.

"Earnie, this is important what I have to tell you," he said in earnest. "You can't drink, smoke, or do drugs, and you must leave the woman alone while training."

I told him I didn't drink, I didn't smoke, and I didn't do drugs. He asked me about women and I just smiled.

"Pedro, I am going to do whatever you say because I want to make it as a fighter," I told him.

The very next morning I started to do roadwork. I ran almost four miles in Packard Park in downtown Warren. I ran early in the morning because the air was fresh. I would get up at 4:30 and be down in the park by 5 o'clock. After I finished running I would go home, eat, shower, and get ready for work. By 7:43, I reported to General Motors for my 8 o'clock shift.

My co-workers soon found out about my new ambition. Not all of them were supportive. One had been an amateur boxer of little note. He warned that I had gotten too late a start in the sport and said a real heavyweight would eat me alive. I believe my enthusiasm made him jealous.

When work was done, I would change and then drive to Youngstown to meet Pedro for an intense workout. After just a week of this I had my first fight.

"Earnie, we were very limited time-wise to prepare for this fight, but with the power that you have in your right hand, all you need is to land it," Pedro instructed. "So, here's the plan: throw a jab, then follow with a fast straight right hand stepping in at the same time."

I made my boxing debut in the 39th annual Golden Gloves tournament held at Struthers Field House in Youngstown on January 17, 1967. A crowd of about 1,500 fans was on hand for the novice division quarter-finals. It was a long night of boxing, and as a heavyweight, my bout would be the last of the evening. Sixteen bouts had taken place when I finally stepped into the ring. It was getting late and I planned to close the show in quick fashion.

Mission accomplished. It was all over at 1:05 of the opening round.

At the bell I came out swinging against my opponent, Noldan Starks. Just seconds later, I put Starks down for an eight-count with a straight right hand. When he regained his footing, I swarmed all over him. I jabbed and threw a right cross that had all my weight behind it. Once again, Starks went down and the referee said no more. This was the high I'd been missing in my 9-5 life. It had been a tremendous night for Pedro, as all eight of his fighters had won in the novice quarter-finals.

The taste of victory was not only sweet, but something I would get accustomed to quickly.

CHAPTER FOUR

Golden Gloves

The following Monday, I returned to the gym filled with high expectations. I was confident of another quick victory in the novice championships.

But then Pedro dropped a bomb on his bomber. Due to my advanced age (22) I had been declared ineligible to compete in the novice division. For a moment it seemed like my boxing career was over after only one bout, but then Pedro said there might be another way. If I were willing, tournament officials would let me fight in the open class with the experienced heavyweights.

All I cared about was getting to fight, so I agreed, even though that put me in the same category as John Henry and 1966 novice 178-pound titlist Mike Boswell, who had grown into a heavyweight. With only one bout to my credit, nobody gave me much of a chance in that league.

My own confidence took a dip when Pedro informed me that he would only be able to work with me on a limited basis prior to my fight because of all the fighters he had competing in the tournament. But he offered me some encouraging words that helped.

"Earnie, the way you can punch, most fighters cannot take it," Pedro said. "Remember to throw your punches at your opponent's neck, because when they see it coming, they will naturally duck to protect their neck, and their chin will lower right on target. That's all I want you to master for now. Do those things well, and you will go a long way."

In the semi-finals of the Golden Gloves, I was originally slated to box James Wade of Warren, but he pulled out at the last minute. So then I was matched with John Henry, the defending champion and the first man I had ever sparred with.

Originally slated to receive a bye, Henry was forced into action when Wade defaulted. Wade was scratched officially due to illness, but I called it cold feet. He was the first of many opponents to come up with an excuse not to get into the ring with me.

In my second amateur bout, I started tossing haymakers at Henry at the opening bell. The first round was give-and-take until I caught him flush near the end of the round. Everybody in the house realized how hard I'd hit him when poor Henry got up and went to the wrong corner between rounds, which drew laughter from the crowd.

Henry was game, again climbing off the canvas in the third round; but I was awarded a unanimous decision. Since our sparring session two weeks earlier, I knew he feared my power. He had politely refused subsequent invitations to join me in the ring. I give him credit for not taking the Wade path out when it counted.

The newspapers started showing interest in me after my second victory. But they misspelled my last name as "Shavers" in all the articles written about me. I didn't mind, and from that point on, it kind of stuck. The mistake even paid off a few years later in court over a contract dispute with boxing promoter Don King.

That rookie year I was runner-up in the Youngstown Golden Gloves heavyweight division. In the finals I lost a three-round decision to Mike Boswell. Boswell also boxed out of my gym. We had never sparred, but I had seen him work. He was a skilled boxer who frustrated me throughout our three-round match. Boswell controlled the fight with his jab, and slid side to side, counter-punching every Hail Mary punch I threw. I realized then that despite my tremendous power I wasn't going to knock out everyone. I also had a difficult time relaxing in the ring. It was a problem that dogged me for most of my fight career.

After three fights and only two weeks as an amateur boxer, I had placed second in the Golden Gloves. I was happy with my initial performance and decided to dedicate myself to my new sport. I realized I was still a novice, and I took every opportunity to learn. In the gym I always had a list of questions for Pedro, but I also learned from the other boxers.

La Verne still wasn't sold on my new career, and the birth of my third daughter, Catherine Denna, on July 15, 1967, seemed to her another pretty good reason for me to stay at home instead of race around the state trying to punch guys out.

A few weeks after the Golden Gloves tournament in Youngstown, I was invited to participate in the regional tournament in Cleveland as an alternate. I never made it, because La Verne tossed all of my boxing equipment in the trunk of my car and then hid the keys. I was mad, but she stood her ground and wouldn't give me the keys until the following day.

La Verne was a strong woman and always did what she felt was in the best interest of the family. But I was upset with her for causing me to miss the fights in Cleveland. We had a long discussion. Finally I convinced her to let me give boxing a try with the hope of someday making the ring my full-time occupation. I was a heavyweight with a sledgehammer for a punch, and there were respected people in the game who felt I had a chance to advance rapidly in this sport. At 22, I didn't have time to waste. La Verne finally understood my passion and acquiesced to my wishes.

I trained with my good friend Richard Austin over that summer. Austin helped me learn the fundamentals of the game. We worked on defense, footwork, and combination punching. I tried to run every morning, too. I was a busy man. I had precious little time to spend with my wife and daughters. In order to open up some free time for the family, I started the 1968 amateur season training at Bob Saffold's gym in Warren to eliminate the commute to Youngstown.

Saffold was a local fireman and a decent guy, but his situation didn't offer the same training opportunities as Pedro Tomez's gym had. Pedro was one of the best amateur coaches in the nation. At his gym he had a seasoned group of boxers to spar with and learn from. Bob didn't have the same talent at his gym. At times Saffold himself would be the only one who dared to spar with me. He used to tell everyone in town that I was responsible for convincing him that putting on the gloves wasn't for him.

While I was working on the line one day, an old professional fighter employed at General Motors bumped into me in the break room. He had heard through co-workers about my amateur success and shared some memories about his brief ring career. He also gave me some advice that helped me pull out some big victories later on. He knew I had intentions of turning professional. He warned that the promoters weren't the only con men in the game.

"One time early in my professional career I was fighting a journeyman boxer who had been on the club-fight circuit for years," he said. "Midway through the first round the journeyman begged to me to go easy on him because he couldn't afford to get knocked out and be put on a 30-day suspension. He had a family to feed. Once he said that, I turned into a sensitive, caring man and started taking it easy on him. As soon as I relaxed, that old-timer tried to take my head off!"

I learned a very valuable lesson from him that day: protect yourself at all times, and in the ring never let anyone off the hook. Sob stories and charity have their time and place, but the ring isn't one of them.

The following year, 1968, I improved tremendously as a boxer. I also experimented more with the power of intimidation. In the Northeastern Golden Gloves tournament in Cleveland, 16 boxers were registered as heavyweights. At the weigh-in I confidently prowled around the room, sizing up each one of my competitors before making an important announcement.

"Nobody is getting out of here alive!" I shouted. The walls had barely stopped reverberating when 11 heavyweights pulled out of the event. One who didn't was Mike Boswell, the man who'd defeated me the year before.

We met again in the finals, after I defeated Canton's Pete Perri to get there. This time, I beat Boswell to win the Youngstown Golden Gloves heavyweight championship. In this fight, unlike our first, I slipped and countered most of Boswell's punches, and was also able to cut off the ring and position him where I wanted him.

Ten members of the Northeastern Ohio Golden Gloves boxing team flew from Cleveland to Salt Lake City for the

National Golden Gloves tournament. With only seven fights, I had to be the least experienced boxer in the tournament, but I defeated Don Foley of Lowell, Massachusetts, in my first bout.

In the quarter-finals I faced Frank Steele of Chicago. Steele had a reputation as one of the best amateurs in the country. Still, I felt confident going in. When the opening bell sounded I took the fight to Steele. I punched for three minutes a round with predictable results. In the third round, I grew weary. I hadn't properly paced myself. Steele came on in the third round and got the decision.

Pedro Tomez was there, but not in my corner. It had been a while since we worked together. In fact, Pedro had been Boswell's cornerman in the Youngstown tournament. I will never forget what he said after the Steele bout.

"Earnie, if you come back to Youngstown and let me train you, I will show you how to win the national AAU tournament in 1969."

With another year of experience under my belt, my name was getting well known and I was improving steadily. In 1969, I handily won the Youngstown, Cleveland, and Ohio tournaments, which included boxers from five other states.

With boxing taking up so much of my free time, I spent whatever was left with La Verne and the girls. It wasn't much. La Verne knew I was working my tail off in the fight game, and she now fully supported my dream of winning security for the family with my fists. I appreciated her vote of confidence.

I was going to be 24 on my next birthday, and knew if I won the national AAU tournament, it would be a springboard to a pro career. I also realized that at my relatively advanced age for an amateur, a poor showing would put me on that assembly line at the plant forever. Factory work is an honest living, but for a dreamer it can be a nightmare.

Two weeks before the tournament, Dave Matthews, a light heavyweight from Akron, and I were invited to attend a professional training camp run by Joey Fariello in upstate New York.

The training camp was in Poughkeepsie, and it was owned by Jimmy Isim, who also owned part of the New York Jets. He wanted to take a look at us because we were getting a reputation as up-and-comers. Isim already owned a piece of professional heavyweight contender Buster Mathis and a few other fighters.

Fariello was the head trainer and the camp director. One of the other fighters training there was John Griffin, a light heavyweight from Cleveland. John and I were good friends and when he told me why I'd been invited to camp, I knew he wasn't shining me on.

"They really want to sign Dave, but in your case, Earnie, they want to make sure you don't win the AAU tournament," Griffin confided. He said what they really wanted to do was sign a white heavyweight by the name of Jimmy Elder. He was the heavyweight champion of the Navy, and they wanted him to win the national AAU tournament for the prestige it would give Elder before they signed him to a contract.

"Everyone knows that the potential marketability of a white heavyweight fighter is worth 10 times that of a black heavyweight fighter when it comes to making money," Griffin said.

Joey Fariello had lured me there so they could check out what kind of fighter I was, as well as do what they could to soften me up for their boy, Elder. Once they saw me in action, they would let Elder and his trainer know how to beat me in the upcoming tournament.

However, they hadn't counted on my pal Griffin's loyalty to a fellow Buckeye.

"We're both from Ohio and we're both trying to make it in the fight game," Griffin said. "So we must look out for one another because these guys sure as hell won't."

Fariello was too busy to work with me in the gym himself, which worked perfectly to my advantage. Griffin had boxed with Elder many times, and we devised a plan whereby he could show me exactly what I needed to do to beat the pride of the Navy without Fariello being any the wiser.

Fariello left camp at 3:30 p.m. every day and came back about two hours later before dinner. Everything was run like clockwork, so our schedule never varied, it was always the same.

Griffin would drop by around 4 p.m. and work with me for an hour, then hightail it out of there before Fariello got back. He didn't want him to know he was helping me out.

"Earnie, the way you can punch, you can knock out Elder by hitting him square on the chin," Griffin said. But he advised me not to trade punches with Elder because he had a lot more experience than I did. And Elder could punch as well. Griffin predicted that the brackets for the tournament would be rigged so that Elder and I would meet in the finals. The promoters knew our fight would create plenty of fireworks.

"Now this is what I want you to do, but do not use it for any other fight except for Elder," Griffin said. He told me to flick my jab like Ali for speed, and hit Elder on the tip of his nose. Flick, then step back and wait five or six seconds before jabbing again, and then, after another brief interlude, a third jab.

"On the third and final jab, flick it, come down off your toes, fall back onto your right heel, and instantly step in, throwing your right hand with all your might, and watch that sucker fall," Griffin said.

For the next 10 days, I worked on this plan every chance I got. By the time the AAU tournament started in San Diego, I was punching harder than I ever had before. I had every move down pat. I stormed through my preliminary opposition. I stopped Morris Hill of Pittsburgh, then KO'd Wayne McGee of New York, and two-time Army champion Otis Evans. That put me in the finals against—guess who—Jimmy Elder.

The bell rang and we both moved toward center ring, circling each other. I threw the first flicking jab, landing on the tip of Elders nose. I stepped back, waited, then moved in and flicked another left jab on Elder's nose. I stepped back again, waited, and threw the third flicking jab. Then I came down off the ball of my foot, falling back onto the heel of my right foot, making me flat footed and ready to unleash every bit of my power.

By then, Elder was mad as hell. He came at me like a runaway tank—or, in his case, aircraft carrier. I stepped in, and, at the same time, threw a hard straight right hand. It connected flush on Elders chin as he came rushing in and down he went as if torpedoed. So much for the New Yorkers' secret plan. And, just like that, I was the national amateur heavyweight champion.

I was so elated that I called La Verne to let her and the girls know what happened as soon as I got back to my room. I told her that I missed them and couldn't wait to get home.

Early the next morning when our plane taxied up the runway, La Verne was waiting for me at the gate. I was so happy to see her and I could not wait to get home and see the girls. My oldest daughter, Tamara, was almost four. Our middle child, Cyndi, was two, and Catherine, the baby, was one. It had been weeks since I was home.

Being a father was wonderful because I got to do things with them. I loved spoiling them, and they certainly didn't mind. In a way, I relived my childhood through them without all the responsibilities I had growing up.

In the fall of 1969, the AAU sent a team to Germany. I fought two fights there, losing once and beating Horst Koscheman, whom I had boxed earlier in Cincinnati. While he beat me in the States, I had the satisfaction of returning the favor in his homeland.

I stayed overseas for a week and loved the German people, customs, and especially their food. The people treated us like champions.

Not long after that, I ended my amateur career with a 20-6 record. Because I had relatively little experience, Pedro felt it wouldn't benefit me to wait for the 1972 U.S. Olympic Trials.

"You have a pro style of fighting, Earnie," he told me. "You'll go much farther if you turn professional rather than wait another three years until the Olympics."

The time had come to take my game to another level.

CHAPTER FIVE

The Pro Ranks

After I won the national AAU heavyweight championship, our lives were never the same. The very next day, the phone started ringing off the hook.

I got calls from such Midwestern promoters as Charlie Harris, Don "The Bomb" Elbaum, and Dean Chance and Blackie Gennaro, along with promoters in other parts of the country.

Legendary Cleveland Brown running back Jim Brown even called and offered his advice on my future career, which came with a curious racial slant.

"You know, Earnie, it might be in your best interest if you went with a white promoter who could advance your career further than I could," Brown said. "Don't sign with any black people. If you do, your career is shot. They can't get you any fights and they're only interested in your money." I've often wondered if he'd take that same stance today with his strong allegiance to the African-American community.

Another call I received soon after the national AAU championships offered a proposition I'll never forget.

"May I speak to Earnie Shavers?" the voice on the other end of the line asked.

"Speaking," I said.

"Would you like to earn $500 by fighting George Foreman on the Joe Frazier vs. Dave Zyglewicz undercard in Houston, Texas, on April 22?" he said, without even bothering to introduce himself. That was breathtaking enough. Then he really got my attention by saying, "But here's the deal: George must win." Foreman had become America's darling by winning the 1968 Olympic heavyweight gold medal and then waving the U.S.

flag in the ring. My anonymous caller explained that what he had in mind was a three-round exhibition between the two top amateur heavyweights in the country. Houston was Foreman's hometown and he would be turning professional shortly.

"You want me to let George Foreman win the fight?" I asked, wanting to make sure our connection wasn't bad.

"Yes," he confirmed

"No, I can't do that," I said politely.

"I'm sorry, we can't use you then. Goodbye."

Click!

A more welcome call came from *Sports Illustrated*. The magazine wanted to do an interview with me for a write-up in its "Faces in the Crowd" column that showcased impressive new athletic talent. They presented me with two awards—a silver plate and a silver dish. After the article came out, the phone calls increased.

I had numerous offers from strangers full of big promises wanting to manage me. Confused, I called Pedro Tomez for advice.

"I've been in the fight game for 50 years, Earnie," he told me. "I have seen all kinds of people come and go in this business and most of them are out to use you if you let them. I will advise you on who to deal with." Tomez warned that there was one guy from Erie, Pennsylvania, who I should definitely stay clear of: a man named Don Elbaum. Pedro said Elbaum would promise me the moon if I went with him, but I would always end up getting the shaft.

"He's not a bad guy," Tomez said, "and he is only trying to survive in the fight game. You can learn a lot from Elbaum, just don't sign anything with him."

Sure enough, Elbaum came knocking on my door with a contract, which I declined to sign. Then Elbaum switched gears, asking if I could help him put up some fight posters around Warren advertising the satellite broadcast of the heavyweight title fight between champion Joe Frazier and Jerry Quarry in June. He promised me $250 to get out 100 posters, and I took the bait. I even took time off from work and busted my tail to put up all 100 posters in just three days. When I finished, I called Elbaum to collect.

"Earnie, I can't pay you the money right now," Elbaum said. In fact, he said that the fight broadcast wouldn't even make it to our area because there wasn't a local tower high enough to pick up the satellite transmission of the fight, or some such silliness. But he was sure sorry. He was definitely going to be sorry the next time I saw him.

"I understand," I said, seething inside. Right then I would have liked to take Mr. Elbaum to the highest tower in Warren, wherever it was, and throw him off it.

They could've beamed that fight off Elbaum's nerve. It towered over everything I could think of, including the Empire State Building. He proved that by asking me to sell tickets for him at the upcoming fight at the Akron Armory. I thought about it and decided it might be an opportunity to blindside him.

Elbaum asked if I'd like $500 worth of tickets to sell or $750 worth. Of course I took the higher amount.

"I guess $750 would be fine for me, Don," I said, trying to hide my snicker. I wanted this white hustler to experience first-hand what we call "Black Man's Revenge."

I went to Akron for the Frazier-Quarry fight broadcast. There were three fights on the undercard, plus a live match featuring one of Elbaum's own fighters, a hometown middleweight named Doyle Baird. Baird won his fight, and afterward he walked up to me to ask for the money from the tickets I'd sold. He explained that his purse was to come out of these proceeds.

"That's too bad, Doyle," I said. "Don owes me some money also. The money from the ticket sales belongs to me, so I'm not going to be able to give it to you."

I could see in his eyes for a split-second that Baird was contemplating having a second, albeit unsanctioned bout that night. But then I appealed to his intelligence.

"Doyle, you are a middleweight and I am a heavyweight," I said. "If you want this money, you're going to have to take it from me." For one of Don Elbaum's fighters, Baird was uncommonly smart. He was also a dangerous man. Baird had fought middleweight champion Nino Bevenuti to a draw the previous year, and before that, he had spent four years in jail for manslaughter. But I didn't care. I wanted my money.

"You're right, Earnie," Baird said. "I don't want it. You keep it. I'll see Don about my money. Goodnight Mr. Shavers."

Who said boxing isn't a civilized sport?

This wasn't the last time I would deal Elbaum. Elbaum was responsible for getting Don King into the fight game. Elbaum assisted King upon his exit from the Marion Correctional Institute in 1971, and would later lead King to me.

Elbaum is one of boxing's true characters. He's been eking out a living on the club fight scene in Ohio and Pennsylvania for years. Elbaum's claim to fame was that he promoted two of Sugar Ray Robinson's final fights, a 10-round victory over Peter Schmidt in Johnstown, Pennsylvania, on October 1, 1965, and a loss to Joey Archer in Pittsburgh on November 10, 1965.

The Johnstown bout took place a few days after what was Sugar Ray's 25th anniversary as a professional fighter. As a publicity gimmick, Elbaum had a cake made to present to Robinson. "Congratulations: 25 Glorious Years," it said. But that wasn't enough for Erie's boy genius. Don also presented Robinson with a box containing two aged boxing gloves. He told Robinson that they were the very gloves Sugar Ray had worn in his professional debut in New York on October 4, 1940. Genuinely touched, Sugar Ray fairly wept his thanks. But then the press asked him to put on the gloves for a touching publicity photo. As Robinson pulled out the gloves, he realized he had been had. Both gloves were left-handed!

Since I had been forewarned about Elbaum's schemes, I searched elsewhere for a manager.

Almost every night, La Verne, Pedro, and I would meet with different people to talk over prospective managers for me. Pedro advised it would be better if I signed with a local manager we knew something about, someone with ties to the community who wouldn't run off with my money.

The three of us finally decided on Joseph "Blackie" Gennaro, a paving contractor from Hillsville, Pennsylvania, about 45 minutes from Warren, and his partner, major league baseball pitcher Dean Chance.

Chance had won the Cy Young Award in 1964, breaking Sandy Koufax's four-year stranglehold on the trophy at a time when baseball had one award winner for both leagues. Dean had gone 20-9 with a low earned-run average of 1.65 and registered 11 shutouts that year. Winner of the 2000 American League Cy Young Award, Pedro Martinez led the big leagues that year with only four shutouts. Salaries have changed, too. Chance had recently signed his most lucrative contract that called for $60,000 a season.

Although still active in baseball after 11 seasons in the major leagues playing baseball for the Los Angeles Angels and the Cleveland Indians, Chance moved back to Wooster, Ohio, and got involved in the fight game. Chance had also promoted fights for heavyweight contender Jerry Quarry. A real point in his favor was that Chance was an arch-enemy of Don Elbaum.

Dean and Blackie already had one fighter under contract, Akron's Ray Anderson, who sported a record of 27-1 and was currently the No. 2 rated light heavyweight in the world. The plan was to have me fight initially on Anderson's undercards as he continued his quest for a title shot.

I could've scored a bigger signing bonus by going elsewhere, but after much soul searching, I knew I had signed with the right people. I received a $3,000 signing bonus and a $200 weekly salary from Gennaro and Chance. Our contract was for three years. Once I signed, I quit my job at the factory. The people at General Motors were supportive and left the door open for my return if the new career path didn't work out. But it was a door I didn't plan to walk back through again.

Gennaro and Chance were stand-up guys who promised not to rush me, but rather to move me along at my own pace so I could get the proper experience. Unfortunately, Dean and Blackie started feuding soon after I turned pro. Dean wanted to do what was best for my career, but Blackie's main concern was the bottom line. He cut corners on training expenses, food, and hotel from the beginning. Blackie wanted to get the money back he invested in me as quickly as possible. I don't think Gennaro realized it cost money to get started in the fight game. Blackie was the financial backer, while Dean did the managing.

"I'm going to be champion of the world someday," I assured La Verne. Ever the realist, she wasn't convinced. She took a job at Packard Electric making wire harnesses for General Motors cars so that one of us would supply a guaranteed steady pay-check. While I was away at training camp, family members pitched in to help with watching the kids so she could work.

The transition from the simon-pure ranks to the pros was an easy one for me. Most of my early paid opponents offered less competition than most amateurs I'd faced.

On November 6, 1969,I had my first professional fight against journeyman Silas "Red" Howell in Akron. Chance and Gennaro promoted the event, and it probably broke even at best. It was difficult turning a profit on the Midwest club circuit. Tickets for the event were priced at $3 for general admission and $7.50 for ringside. I felt confident. I knew my style was better suited to the pro game. I knew I was only a punch away from victory.

A lot of family members and friends came out for my pro debut. I had already developed a good following, and I gave my fans something to cheer about by knocking out Howell in the second round. The highlight of the Akron card was the homecoming of local contender Ray Anderson. Anderson had relocated to Minneapolis for training purposes, and the arena exploded when he made his grand entrance. Ray didn't disappoint, knocking out Joe Byrd in the first round. Anderson then tossed his gloves into the crowd and told the press that he planned to bring a world championship to his deserving Ohio fans. It was hard to upstage that.

Later that evening, I attended the post-fight party. Anderson was dressed in a hot pink suit and his coat was adorned with wide mink lapels. He had confided to me that he had designed it himself. Next time, Anderson promised, his suit would have chinchilla lapels.

Mr. Blackwell might have disapproved, but I thought Anderson looked like a million bucks because he was on his way to a title shot. This was my first glimpse into the high life of professional boxing, and I took it all in with wide-eyed wonder.

I hardly had time to savor the victory because my second professional fight was five days later on November 11, in Orlando, Florida, against George Holden. Chance knew a lot of people and he wanted me to get exposure all over the country. He kept me on a whirlwind pace. After knocking out Holden in one round we caught the next flight out of town for Seattle to fight again two days later. Three fights in three different states in eight days. Too bad I was on a straight salary.

Dean was billing me as the "Black Destroyer," complete with a shiny new robe bearing my fight name. The great dream in boxing is to find the "Great White Hope," and Dean told everybody who'd listen I was the guy who would destroy that hope.

On November 13, I fought Stan Johnson, and lost a four-round split decision. I cut both of Johnson's eyes, but couldn't land a fight-ending blow.

A small heavyweight, Johnson used his experience against me by moving around behind a flicking jab. I had trouble cutting off the ring and I chased him around all night. Pedro kept telling me that I wasn't going to knock out everybody that I fought, and I was finding out how right he was. He said that I needed more experience so that when I did meet a skilled opponent, I would know how to handle him.

"This is a part of life," Pedro said of my first defeat. "You must take the bitter as well as the sweet things in life."

A week later, I was back in action in yet another state. This time I fought in Rapid City, South Dakota. It had been over a decade since this area had seen any live professional boxing. Apparently the locals hadn't seen somebody with my appetite in a long time, either. When I ordered six eggs for breakfast on the morning of the fight, the waitress at the restaurant reacted as if I had said I wanted to eat her bee-hive hairdo.

Once again, Ray Anderson headlined the show. Always playing the angles, Dean told the local media that if Anderson won the light heavyweight title they might promote a world-title defense right there in Rapid City. I just couldn't picture it. Where would the ring be? In the middle of a cornfield?

Anderson dazzled the crowd with a stellar performance. I wasn't so bad myself, blasting out Lee Roy in three rounds.

Two weeks later I was back in Ohio to fight 2-0 J.D. McCauley. I'd already beaten him in the amateurs, and figured to make it two in a row over him without too much trouble. McCauley had a nephew named James "Buster" Douglas, who would one day shock the world by winning the heavyweight title from Mike Tyson. Later, McCauley became Douglas' trainer.

J.D. had a fighting style similar to Joe Frazier, always bent over and coming at you. In the second round I hit him with a jab, followed with a right uppercut and topped it off with a left hook. The uppercut did the most damage, knocking McCauley's teeth through his lower lip. He was out on his feet. When the referee saw all the blood, he stepped in and pointed McCauley in the direction of the nearest hospital.

My last fight that year was a four-round decision win against Bill Wilson on December 27. With that, I had gone a total of 20 rounds in eight fights in seven weeks.

My managers kept me busy. They promoted many of my fights themselves in order to get me the experience I needed, even though it meant taking a financial beating on most of the promotions. It's extremely difficult to turn a profit at the club fight level, but Dean saw the big picture and planned to shoot for the bigger payoff when he felt I was ready. However, Blackie was getting frustrated with all the red ink and wanted to see a quick return on his investment. On top of that, Blackie's wife hated the fight game and was putting pressure on him to get his money back ASAP.

Dean brought in top professional fighters to spar with me in the gym. I gained a lot of experience working with these guys because they would show me my mistakes and work with me until I got it right. Ray Anderson tried to get me to relax more in the ring. Anderson also taught me the heart punch. If you connect with a solid hit under your opponent's heart, the effects will linger and take their toll on him during a fight.

At the beginning of 1970, I knocked out Tiger Brown twice in January, and in-between KO'd Joe Byrd, the father of former heavyweight contender Chris Byrd. The second fight with Brown introduced me to the seedy side of professional boxing.

After easily icing him in the opening round in our initial contest, I was surprised to hear that he would be facing me again 20 days later. In fact, Brown was the one who approached Dean about the fight because he needed the money to pay rent. It's a shame that in the fight game there's so many of these types of fighters who seemed to live below the poverty level. But at the time I tried not to feel sorry for any of them, because I realized that they would knock my head off given the opportunity. That's why I never totally depended on boxing as my only source of income. I always kept something going on the side in case something happened.

It didn't take me long to realize that only about one percent of all fighters make enough money in the game to support themselves. If they have no plans for their lives after the gloves come off for good, they lose their purpose in life. I've seen too many boxers become destitute and end up in bad health from alcohol and substance abuse because they never looked beyond the ropes.

Shortly after stopping Brown again, Chance told me that he was sending me back to Peers Training Camp in upstate New York. My old pal Joey Fariello was personally going to train me—this time to win. It was about time.

Fariello was a disciple of Cus D'Amato, the crafty, eccentric genius who had guided Floyd Patterson to the heavyweight throne and later would develop Mike Tyson. This would be an excellent opportunity to advance my career. There were some experienced fighters in camp willing to help me. I would only have to concentrate on boxing.

I told La Verne I would be gone for a few weeks. Little did I know that most of the next two years of my life would be spent in training camps around the country.

I flew into New York City, then took a train to Poughkeepsie. Fariello was there to pick me up and drive me back to camp. The camp was on a farm with 100 acres of land and a very large lake to fish in. Once I saw the lake, I felt right at home.

Fariello introduced me to everyone there, and in a few days I felt comfortable and at ease with all the other fighters. My good friend and confidant John Griffin from Cleveland was still there. John had fought in the main event when I beat J.D. McCauley, and we remained in touch. He had moved to an apartment in Poughkeepsie so he could be closer to the camp.

Also at the camp was another good friend, Dave Matthews, from Akron. Matthews won the national AAU light heavyweight championship the same year I took the heavyweight honors and we both boxed on the same pro card.

Training camp was an entirely new world for me. The first thing I learned was that top fighters spend about 18 hours a day in bed resting. Fariello laid down some ground rules as I laced on the gloves for the first time.

"If you are looking for longevity in the fight game, you must learn to live right, and living right means taking good care of yourself," he said. "I am not here to guard you. You must want this for yourself more than I want it for you."

Then Fariello ticked off a laundry list of items I needed to know in order to succeed in boxing. First, he emphatically advised no drugs or alcohol. Eat the proper food, get plenty of rest, and absolutely no women while in training.

Everything would be done on a schedule: In bed nightly by 10 o' clock and up at 4:30 a.m. Start road work by 5 a.m. and run between five to seven miles. Come home, wash up, get back in bed. Get up again at 8:30, have breakfast at 9, then go for a two-mile walk. The walk helps to digest the food. Get back to bed and rest until 12:30 in the afternoon. Training began at 1 o' clock for two hours. At 3, take a shower, the only shower for the day. (Too much hot water saps body strength over time.)

But Fariello wasn't totally concerned about my welfare. He still harbored a grudge over what I'd done to Jimmy Elder. Turned out that Elder was also in camp then, trying to work past what I'd done to him in San Diego.

My friend Griffin pulled me aside to tell me that Fariello was up to his old tricks, and I should watch out for him and Elder.

I had been in camp only two days when Fariello asked if I wanted to box Elder.

"Yes," I said, to his considerable surprise. Clearly, he had expected me to turn the offer down because new arrivals were not expected to box in the first week there.

I had my gloves put on first purposely, so I could go in the ring and move around to get loose, but also to show Elder I was looking forward to laying more leather on him. I learned that boxing is as much mental as it is physical, and many of the battles are won even before a fighter steps into the ring.

When the bell rang, we picked up right where we left off in California. Even with the big gloves on, I had too much fire-power for Elder. I was dealing out some of my best licks, and Fariello jumped into the ring and pulled me off his boy right away. Elder was out.

"This is the last time you two will ever box," said Fariello, foiled again. But do you want to hear something surprising? After that, Elder and I became very good friends. He was the only boxer in camp with his own car. He would often give me a lift into town. We trained in the gym many times together, but, true to Fariello's word, we never boxed again. Elder's contract was sold to a rival promoter a year after I arrived, and I never saw him again. I took it very hard when he died a year later of brain cancer.

Boxing, I discovered, carried with it a very heavy price. Of the 88 opponents I faced as a pro, more than half are either dead, destitute, or in jail.

CHAPTER SIX

Gym Wars

After all the political machinations played out, we became a tight-knit family unit at camp. We even had our own camp cook, a lady from New York City we called "Mom." She'd come up for the week and leave on weekends.

At 6 p.m. sharp, I ate supper, which usually consisted of steak and green vegetables. We avoided soda pop and anything fried. We drank a little milk, because too much of it would make it difficult to breathe. Dinner was followed by another two-mile walk. After that, I was free to do as I wished. Usually, that meant fishing, watching a movie, reading a book, or going shopping. Regardless of what I did, I had to be in bed by 9:30 p.m.

Despite the rigid lifestyle of training camp, I really enjoyed the feeling of having a goal and working toward it. Being with all the other fighters, swapping war stories and hearing about others' experiences in the fight game nurtured my soul. More than anything, I enjoyed the friendship that formed between fighters.

I lived in a boarding house with 5-10 other fighters. We stayed in one big main house. We played cards and listened to music. I listened to the Temptations and other Motown bands. We played Blackjack and Crazy Eights for fun because none of us had any cash to gamble with. I also did a lot of reading—mostly biographies of other fighters. My favorite book was a biography of Joe Louis. Ironically, he was a distant relative of La Verne's. (My first mother-in-law's stepbrother, to be exact.)

I missed my family and placed a picture of La Verne and the girls on my dresser at camp. I thought of them daily and phoned home frequently.

One of my fondest pastimes was fishing in the big lake. Big Buster Mathis was training in the camp next to ours, at Cus D'Amato's place about five miles away. Buster loved to fish as much as I did, and he was good at it. We tried to get together a few times a month. We caught mostly large-mouth bass, which were great eating.

The first 10 days of camp, I chopped down large trees for 45 minutes a day and used the wood in the fireplace. The chopping added that extra snap in the wrist for punching power, and it made a big difference in the ring. I knocked out Art Miller in one and almost killed the next man who entered the ring with me.

I returned to action in Youngstown, Ohio. The Youngstown boxing community was proclaiming that hometown prospect Ted Gullick was the next heavyweight champion. But after breaking Ray Asher's jaw with a right hand, and later flooring him with another right, I gave the local fans something to think about.

After crunching a few more no-hopers in Ohio, I signed to fight another rising contender, undefeated Ron Stander, in his own backyard, Omaha, Nebraska. Stander's slate stood at 9-0, but I was ready for the step-up in class. I knew I had to score a knockout, because if Stander was still standing at the end there wouldn't be much chance of me getting the decision in his hometown.

Like me, Stander had turned pro in 1969. We had a mutual opponent in Joe Byrd, who I had stopped, while Stander won a six-round decision over him. Big Ron, who was called the "Bluffs Butcher," was a stocky White Hope who liked to wade into his opponents throwing bombs and maul them around. Our fight was set for May 12.

Dean was pitching with the Cleveland Indians then and would not be in Omaha. But he still managed to help build the gate from afar.

"They [the Omaha fans] won't be disappointed this time," he said, referring to Stander's last two less-than enthralling hometown performances. "The winner of this fight will be going for the heavyweight title someday. I'm taking a helluva gamble and so is Dick Noland [Stander's manager]—these are two of the best young heavyweights in the country."

Dean was as good at pitching the hype as he was at throwing the horsehair.

"I'm surprised he took this fight," he said of Noland. "It's a cardinal rule that you never put a young fighter like Stander in with a puncher. And there is nobody tougher than Shavers. Anybody he can hit, he can take out. And Stander comes at his opponents, which is just the way Shavers likes them."

I told the press that the Bluffs Butcher was dead meat, and said I planned to slice him up in five. I was photographed in the *Omaha World-Herald* newspaper offices holding up my fist to a picture of Stander.

Stander's head was as hard as Italian marble. I built up a lead in the first two rounds. Every time Stander even started to punch, the crowd reacted with raucous whoops.

In the third round, I broke my right hand punching that impregnable corn-fed noggin. My hands had been wrapped too tightly before the bout. Due to our small expense budget, I was not able to have Pedro flown in for the bout to work with me.

The pain was overwhelming, but I tried to keep punching. But with just one good hand, I was only half as effective as before. That's when the tide turned in Stander's favor. And I'll be honest—the guy could whack, too. At the beginning of the fifth round, my corner threw in the towel and Stander received a technical knockout victory. It was the first time somebody beat me using his head as a deadly weapon.

After a three-month layoff to let my hand heal, I wanted a rematch with Stander. He'd gotten $450 for our fight, but now his asking price was $12,000. Seems that a victory over me raised his stock in the boxing world quite a bit.

The upside of the defeat, if there was one, was that I had the opportunity to go home and spend some time with La Verne and the girls. I had missed them, and being around them lifted my spirits. Time with my family was always well spent, and they could heal all my cuts and bruises from the ring.

It was hard to swallow the loss to Stander because I was riding an 11-fight win streak and getting more attention than ever. At the end of those three months I was itching to make up for lost time, and when the hand was right, I would go on one of the longest knockout streaks in heavyweight history.

But as my hand healed, my management team began to fracture. Dean Chance and Blackie Gennaro were at war constantly, and finances were the bone of contention. Chance knew it took money to make money, but Gennaro keep looking for that instant jackpot.

Dean had laid out an agenda for my career aimed at a world title fight. He knew I wasn't ready for top challengers at this stage in my career. Ted Gullick, however, was a different story.

Gullick, out of Cleveland, had captured a national title as an amateur and was having a good run in the pro ranks. He was on a 10-bout knockout streak when—with a little prodding from Chance—everyone in Ohio started calling for a Shavers-Gullick fight.

Dean's anticipation of the match probably had more than a little to do with the fact that Gullick was promoted by Don Elbaum. Their ongoing feud could be humorous at times. Elbaum, no shrinking violet, once even called Dean out in the ring. Dean gave it some consideration but knew he would stand a better chance throwing baseballs at Elbaum's melon from 60 feet.

Chance had connections everywhere, and he also wanted me to start getting some exposure in Las Vegas. He boasted that within a year I would be fighting for the Nevada heavyweight title. I had to remind him that I had never even been to Nevada.

To start things heating up for my fight against Gullick, we both shared top billing in a card at Fitch Stadium in Youngstown. In his fight, Gullick laid out Joe Byrd in two. Then he grabbed the microphone and announced that he wanted to get me into the ring real soon. My fists were even more eloquent that night, as I needed just 42 seconds to blast out Jim Daniels.

Gullick and I were friendly enemies. We respected each other's abilities as fighters and never let it get personal. Gullick was originally from Youngstown, and had won the national AAU title in 1963. He was a few years older than me and had always been helpful when we trained in the same gym.

We even held a few public workouts together in a nearby mall to help build the gate for our joint appearance at Fitch Stadium. I really liked Gullick, but we both realized Ohio wasn't big enough for two big-punching heavyweights. It would be over a year before we finally squared off, though, because Chance and Elbaum couldn't come to a mutual agreement on several key issues.

In the meantime I kept busy. Less than two weeks after the Daniels blowout, I knocked out Don Branch in one round in Columbus.

My next bout was against Johnny Hudgins, a protege of famous trainer Angelo Dundee and a sparring partner of Muhammad Ali. Hudgins' resume included a convincing 10-round decision over Ted Gullick. On paper it seemed like a stern test, but it was over in less than 90 seconds, with Hudgins laid out by my right hand.

My fame was spreading. A few days after the fight I received an invitation to appear on the undercard of Ali's bout against Argentine strong man Oscar Bonavena, seven weeks later at Madison Square Garden. But first came Sonny Liston's one-time sparring partner Johnny Mac in Youngstown.

Our bout at the Fitch High Fieldhouse was held before the closed-circuit TV broadcast of heavyweight champ Joe Frazier's title defense against 175-pound Bob Foster from Detroit. After I stopped Mac in four rounds, I hung around to watch Frazier annihilate Foster in a one-sided affair.

My win over Mac gave my friend Dick Olmstead, a sportswriter for the *Warren-Tribune Chronicle*, bragging material for his cronies in New York. The latter were anxious to get a look at the big, black, Buckeye wonder they'd heard so much about.

My opponent for my Gotham debut was undefeated Bunky Akins, who was recently named "Prospect of the Month" by *The Ring* magazine. He was also a sparring partner for Ali. Not only was I the underdog against him, but I would also have to fight my fear of crowds that would undoubtedly rear up more than ever at Madison Square Garden. The last thing I needed was to freeze up in my first shot at boxing's big time.

It was Ali's second fight since his return from the exile imposed by his conviction—finally overturned by the U.S. Supreme Court—for evading the draft. The Reverend Jesse Jackson, a friend of Ali's, was omnipresent, proclaiming that Ali represented a champion of manhood.

"For him [Ali] to have forgone the money and to risk going to jail, which appears inevitable, for his principles—this puts him in the tradition of Socrates and Dr. King, which is more than being a boxer," Jackson sermonized. "He hasn't let his ideas be polluted by the price of fame."

It was a super-charged atmosphere, and I did my best to soak it up. Celebrities like Dustin Hoffman and Woody Allen popped up everywhere. Coming from the Midwest club circuit, this was quite an eye-opener for this Ohio hayseed.

At a press conference, Ali talked of meeting Joe Frazier for the heavyweight title. In fact, he was more concerned about Frazier than about Bonavena. When he wasn't calling for Frazier's blood, Ali would shout, "Bonavena will be mine in nine." That was a bold prediction considering that nobody had ever stopped the hard-headed Argentinean. Even Frazier had been taken the distance by Bonavena, and put on the floor twice by him, to boot.

Ali was the master of hype and his return pumped new life into the sport of boxing. At the time, he and I weren't even acquaintances, but I respected what he did for the sport. Soon enough we would become friends, and then opponents. I sure enjoyed getting a first-hand glimpse of the legend in action.

I also enjoyed witnessing the birth of my fourth daughter, Carla, on December 1, 1970, six days before my next fight on Pearl Harbor Day. For poor Bunky Akins, it was a day of personal infamy. Fifty-nine seconds into our fight, it was over. I knocked him down twice, the second time with a right uppercut that put him out cold. I was obviously relaxed and felt in complete control.

Previously, I had put myself under unnecessary pressure, even in workouts when someone was watching. I had the necessary killer instinct, and with every punch I thought of massacring the other guy. But I tried so hard that I'd tighten up, miss some shots, and then, with one eye to the onlookers, try too hard to get on track. Working out with Mike Boswell a couple of weeks, listening to Pedro's advice in the gym, and taking tips from the New York fight fraternity, I learned how to take "cool" control in the ring. No longer did I try to annihilate every sparring partner. I concentrated on taking care of business on my side of the ropes, and let the crowd take care of itself.

One bad thing that came out of the Akins victory was that Pedro and I went our separate ways. The entire time I had been training in New York, he was noticeably absent. Ostensibly it was because his main responsibility was with his amateur fighters. But the real problem between us was money.

Pedro wanted 10 percent of my purses even though he was never in training camp with me. The people who did train me also wanted 10 percent, and then Dean and Blackie took their cut. After Uncle Sam collected his share of the pie, there wasn't much left for me, the guy who was taking all the punches.

I was willing to give Pedro 10 percent of my purse for every fight he worked with me. That was more than reasonable, I thought, but we were both stubborn and neither of us would budge. So it was goodbye. We remained on friendly terms, but Pedro was now permanently absent from my corner.

Ironically, Pedro confided to a few associates that he made more money with me than he had with any other boxer. It's too bad that money had to undermine such a good working relationship, because his knowledge was an asset to me.

The day after the Akins fight, the headline in the *Youngstown Vindicator* read: "Shavers scored a brilliant TKO at the Garden over Bunky Akins."

Dean knew that I was ready to start making my move up the heavyweight ranks. *Boxing Illustrated* produced a list of their top 50 heavyweights, and my former gym mates Ted Gullick and Dave Matthews were listed 41st and 46th, respectively. I knew I wasn't too far from joining them on the list.

I had been in Peers Training Camp for 18 months when Dean Chance suggested I move out west to California. That was fine with me, especially when I found out that Chance planned to hook me up with veteran trainer Willie Ketchum at Los Angeles' famed Main Street Gym.

Ketchum was an old-timer who had trained former world featherweight champion Davey Moore and lightweight king Jimmy Carter. Since the plans called for California, Dean introduced me to his favorite Hollywood playboy, baseball pitcher Bo Belinsky. Belinsky had made headlines throughout his playing career, more for his off-the-field antics and Hollywood romances than his baseball deeds. His favorite pastime and the national pastime would never be confused.

Belinsky had showed signs of brilliance early in his career. He pitched a no-hitter in his rookie season with the California Angels. Apparently, though, he never struck out in the bedroom, and Bo's romances with Hollywood sex kittens Ann-Margret, Tina Louise, and Mamie Van Doren were routine tabloid fodder. His brief marriage to Van Doren was considered one of baseball's most publicized celebrity marriages, finishing a distant second to Joe DiMaggio and Marilyn Monroe. It would be more than 25 years later when the brief Jose Canseco-Madonna fling made as many tabloid headlines.

Belinsky had been a teammate of Dean's with the Angels, and the two remained close friends. The way Chance told it, on the ballclub he really roomed with Bo's suitcase.

Belinsky's pitching career was over when the Cincinnati Reds released him in the fall of 1970. Bo's marriage to gorgeous Playboy Playmate Jo Collins wasn't far behind. Chance knew his friend was struggling and tried to include him in our boxing plans. Dean himself had just been traded to the New York Mets, but that didn't keep him from full-time involvement in my career.

In my first Las Vegas appearance on the road west, I boxed Lee Estes in the "Strip Fight of the Week" at the Silver Slipper, with my new corner crew of Willie Ketchum and Bo Belinsky. I impressed Ketchum by taking Estes out in two, and Belinsky harkened back to his diamond days to assess my performance.

"That guy hits like some of the fellows who tagged me," he quipped.

Bo was a cool guy, but the last thing I needed was to start hanging with him. I was usually waking up for morning roadwork when he was coming home. But he was always fun to have around.

George Foreman had been bowling over everybody he fought, and we figured it was time to give him a taste of his own medicine.

"We want Foreman," Chance announced. "And I've offered him $25,000 to meet Shavers, but all of a sudden Foreman's people have got hearing problems. They can't hear me on the phone and can't read either. I mean, the numerous wires and letters I sent them should have commanded a response. But, our time is coming, you just wait and see."

Old Cy Young himself couldn't have pitched it much straighter than that.

CHAPTER SEVEN

Showdown

Ketchum liked what he saw of me against Estes, but he was uncertain about taking over my training duties because he already had a heavyweight prospect of his own in Richard Gosha, out of Chicago. The surest way I knew how to come out on top in that sweepstakes was over Gosha's unconscious body.

"Whip him and Ketchum will train you," Chance said. So I whipped him but good. I became the first professional fighter to knock Gosha off his feet, but he was no tomato can or card-carrying member of the Bum-of-the-Month-Club. He was the toughest opponent of my career up to then.

We fought at the Akron Armory on February 17, 1971. I won the first two rounds, but Gosha was a gutsy fighter with a 22-9 record. He came on strong in the third and fourth with body punches that were hard to weather, but I managed. In the fifth I started to unload on Gosha.

I had him down before referee Doc Holloway raised my hand at 2:38 of the fifth round.

The Gosha fight had been an action-packed war. I had battled a cold the week before the fight that had sapped some of my strength. When the fight was over I lay on the dressing room table for a long time, totally exhausted.

It was great to be back in Ohio, seeing my girls. I had really missed them. Sometimes I felt like a selfish person, off doing what I wanted instead of staying home like other husbands and dads. But I knew that big paydays were just around the comer. La Verne's support meant everything. Her brother, Vernice Payne, lived in Los Angeles and I stayed with him when I hit town.

With Gosha out of the picture, Willie Ketchum became my trainer. When I wasn't fighting, I would work out every afternoon from 1 to 3 o'clock at the fabled Main Street Gym.

The grimy old gym sat atop an old movie theater and was located in the heart of Los Angeles' skid row. It was a genuine hole in the wall. A sign above the entrance read: "World Rated Boxers Train Here Daily." There should have been another sign that read, "The scourge of the earth live here."

Los Angeles had lots of boxing gyms but none with the history of Main Street, or its reputation for producing some great fighters. Over the years boxing immortals like Jack Johnson, Rocky Marciano, and Sugar Ray Robinson had passed through its doors.

The gym was owned by Howie Steindler, a feisty old-timer who ran the place with an iron fist. He kept a lock on his phone in the gym's office and a billy club hanging on the wall in case there was trouble. I couldn't see anybody giving Steindler a hard time, much less put in a request to use his phone.

Like many tough guys, Steindler also had a softer side to him that people rarely saw. Homeless people often wondered into the gym and Steindler would tactfully escort them out, but on rainy days he'd allow them to seek refuge there.

One story concerning Steindler and my future opponent, Jerry Quarry, still gives me the giggles. Quarry worked out at the Main Street Gym on weekends because his regular gym was dosed on Saturdays and his entire family liked to come by and watch. It was some family. Jerry's parents, brothers, sisters, and children would fill the bleachers at one end of the gym. His mother would pack a picnic basket and the family would make an event of it, to the constant irritation of Steindler.

One day after the Quarrys left the gym, Howie had to pick up the paper plates, cups, and napkins they'd left behind. The gruff little dude finally posted another sign by the front door that read, "THIS IS A BOXING GYM. IF YOU WANT TO HAVE A PICNIC, TAKE IT TO GRIFFITH PARK."

Years later, scenes from the first three *Rocky* films were shot at Main Street. The word was that Rocky Balboa's trainer in the movie, Mickey (brilliantly portrayed by Burgess Meredith), was based on Steindler himself.

After starting my workouts at the gym, I was introduced to Sugar Ray Robinson. I was working out when a trainer at the gym introduced me to him.

"Earnie Shavers, I heard of you, you're that great puncher from Ohio," said the former welterweight and middleweight champ, considered by many experts as the greatest boxer ever. Ego boosts don't come any bigger than that.

Robinson asked me about an old Youngstown boxer, Tommy Bell, who he beat for the 147-pound title. I told him that I knew Bell quite well and that he had always been proud to go the distance twice with the "Great Sugar Ray." He just smiled.

While I trained at the Main Street Gym, Robinson from time to time gave me pointers that helped me in my climb up the heavyweight ladder.

"When you stop getting nervous before a fight, quit because you're crazy," he told me. "I don't care how long you've been in it—you're always supposed to be nervous before a fight."

Mac Foster was another KO artist training at Main Street. He'd moved down from Fresno in search of quality sparring. I was in the market myself, so Ketchum asked Foster's trainer if it would be OK for us to spar together. Foster and his trainer agreed so fast they must have figured me for a pushover.

That impression was confirmed when Foster tried to knock me out in the first round.

"When you get a chance, let him feel your power," Ketchum said when I got back to my corner. He also advised me to try to smother Foster to prevent him from utilizing his full power.

The second round we both got a little hot-headed, jockeying for position. Foster was much bigger and taller, but I punched harder and faster. When Foster jabbed, I would slip inside his punch and at the same time throw a hard right to the body. Then I came back with a left hook to the jaw, followed by a fast right. I knew I hurt him, and his trainer grabbed Foster to keep him from falling.

After a short break, Foster regained his composure and we resumed sparring. Foster wound a big right hand, but I beat him to the punch with my own jab. Foster tried his own jab, but I slipped it and threw two left hooks, one to the body and the second to the head, followed by a right hand that tore his headgear off. He was hurt bad and his trainer stepped in and stopped us. The next day Foster went back to Fresno.

The wins that counted on my resumé kept coming, too. After two quick KOs in Las Vegas and another in Akron, I flew down to Tampa, Florida, to fight on the undercard of Ray Anderson's challenge for the light heavyweight title held by hard-banging Bob Foster. Foster had held the title for three years and had never been beaten by a light heavyweight. At the weigh-in, Anderson got under Foster's skin by boasting about what he'd do in the ring.

"I'm gonna yell when I punch," Ray said, adding, "I shouldn't tell this, but Foster is too dumb to pick it up, so it won't matter."

"If I get any madder I might just carry him and beat the hell out of him for 15 rounds," Foster retaliated. It was kind of a lesson in what not to do against a legitimate superstar like Foster. He had defended his title five times and wasn't about to be intimidated by Anderson's jive talk. Foster was a 3-1 favorite.

Ray also needled Foster about his recent knockout loss to Joe Frazier in a bid for the heavyweight title. Ray's contract with Dean Chance had been recently sold to Yank Durham, "Smokin'" Joe's manager and trainer. Frazier was scheduled to be in Anderson's corner for the title shot. I really thought Ray had an excellent chance to win the title because he was so talented. Dean Chance had often said that Ray had the skills to be the next Sugar Ray Robinson.

Four years earlier, after a 1967 Anderson victory in San Francisco, legendary former light heavyweight champion Archie Moore wrote Ray a brief note that said, "You'll be the light heavyweight champion in three years. Easy." Archie himself was on hand to provide the color commentary for the Foster-Anderson telecast aired over American Telesports Network. At the time I had no way of knowing that the "Ole Mongoose" would one day become my trainer.

I admired Bob Foster as a fighter, but my rooting interest was in Anderson. Ray was a personal friend. He had also escaped the "Deep South" of Alabama and relocated to Ohio. After I took out Willie Johnson in four in a preliminary match, I grabbed a seat for the title fight.

It was a let-down as Anderson dropped a unanimous 15-round decision to Foster. As if losing wasn't bad enough, for his shot at glory Ray grossed only $20,000. That was before Uncle Sam and his management got their piece of the action. It made me feel fortunate to be a heavyweight. I knew I had a shot at some bigger dollars.

The experience of being involved in another championship card was beneficial, but I felt for my friend Ray. He taught me the importance of taking care of yourself. Unfortunately, with Ray it was a case of, "Do as I say, not as I do." Ray always enjoyed the night life. I remember hearing stories of when Ray trained in Minneapolis and would visit Dean when he was pitching with the Twins. Ray had an apartment in the same complex as Twins hitting sensation Rod Carew. But I guess it was Twins manager Billy Martin who Anderson really hit it off with. Maybe all those wild nights had caught up to Ray by the time he fought Bob Foster. After the loss to Foster, Anderson never again came close to another title shot. He became a journeyman and a sparring partner for hire. Ray taught me plenty of moves to copy inside the ropes, and quite a few to avoid outside the ring.

My record now stood at 26-2, all my wins by knockout; I had stopped my last 14 foes. Chuck Leslie was number fifteen on my hit parade. He had fought some of the top fighters, including Joe Frazier, Ron Lyle, Bob Foster, Ken Norton, and Jimmy Ellis. Leslie had a reputation as a spoiler who could make anybody look bad, but early in the fight I knocked him through the ropes and closed his right eye. In the tenth, I hit him with a right hand on the injured eye and he fell through the ropes by his own corner and was counted out. It was the very first time in 25 knockout victories that I had to go more than five rounds.

Four weeks later, I returned to Warren to a warm homecoming, as if I was already the heavyweight champion. Pedro agreed to work my corner against last-minute substitute Bill Hardney. He was only too happy to get his 10 percent of my purse, and to expound on my prospects in an interview with the *Youngstown Vindicator*.

"Most of the journeymen seconds are just doing a job, they don't understand the boxer, they just want to get the bout over," Pedro said. "So they yell, 'Knock him out,' and Earnie listens, tries to land his TNT wallop on everyone. They should be cautioning him to stay loose, do some boxing. It's when you try for a quick KO you get tired and tense. Shavers is a tremendous boxer, has a beautiful left and I hope the fans around here really get out and see what a future champion they have in their midst. I'll be in his corner in Warren."

I spent the day before the fight fishing with my girls. They really loved it, and every outing I had with them made me work that much harder in the ring. It had been a long time since I had been able to spend some quality time with them.

I sure didn't spend much time with Hardney. I blitzed him in one round and then was mobbed for about 15 minutes as I tried to make my way out of the ring. I donated my purse to the Varsity House fund—after paying Pedro his cut, of course.

Hardney got even with me for the fight, although it took him over 20 years. He introduced me to a crazy woman in Colorado who briefly became my wife. More on that later.

After two more quick victories, I signed to fight for the heavyweight championship of Nevada. I guess I qualified by having fought in the state four times. In the other corner would be Irish Pat Duncan, with Reno the site of our encounter.

Fighting in Nevada was quite different than the Ohio club shows. I boarded a bus jammed with tourists. During the 45-minute ride to our hotel, scantily dressed waitresses served cocktails to party-going tourists. I just tried to relax amidst the revelry.

Chance and I, along with sparring partner Don Taylor, arrived in town early to adjust to the altitude. When I fought Leslie in Lake Tahoe, the altitude gave me problems because I hadn't been there long enough to get adjusted to the thin air. By the eighth round I was pretty winded. I wasn't going to make the same mistake twice.

Duncan was from Carson City, Nevada, the state capitol, and if the fight went the distance, I wasn't going to get the decision. My job would be to keep the pressure on until he dropped.

The opening PR salvo was fired by Duncan's manager, Ted Walker, who told the local press that I was a dirty fighter. That was a new one on me. I certainly didn't consider myself that, nor did anyone else in the boxing profession. I fought the only way I knew how: hard and relentless. I didn't give anybody any breaks. If that's what made me a dirty fighter, then I guess I was dirty. My printable answer to the charge was that Duncan would pay in the ring for it.

I trained at the Mapes Hotel Casino lounge for two hours a day to help build interest at the gate. The place was full of boxing fans and blue-haired old ladies. Lawrence Welk was the other entertainment at the hotel.

The day of the fight, I tipped the scales at a lithe 204 pounds. Duncan weighed four pounds less, but was two inches taller. He used his height and reach advantage well in the first four rounds that night. He jabbed effectively and kept me at bay. But in the fifth, I got Duncan against the ropes and blasted him to the canvas with a right hand and left hook. Jim Davis, the University of Nevada boxing coach, took one look at Duncan as he lay quivering and told referee John McSweeney that the fight was all over for his boy.

Duncan stayed on the deck for five minutes. I liked to put a man to sleep, but 10 seconds was long enough. The idea that I might cause serious injury with my power had crossed my mind, but hell, I was taking the same risk myself every time I got in the ring.

After three more victories in October and November, I had a few weeks off to spend time with La Verne and the girls over the holidays.

Come the new year, I had a date with Ted Gullick.

A huge advantage I had going in against my Ohio rival was Pedro, who had trained Gullick since the latter was a kid, but would be with me in the fight because of that ever-loving 10 percent. It entitled me to everything Pedro knew about Gullick.

"I know all of his weaknesses and I'm going to show you how to beat him," Pedro said. "This fight is a must-win for you. So when you win, I win also."

The fight was billed as Ohio's own version of Ali vs. Frazier. I didn't know which one I was supposed to be, but I knew I was going to be the last one standing.

I set up camp in Poughkeepsie under Joey Fariello. A week later, who should show up there but Gullick himself. No big deal. We were good friends and even ended up doing our road-work together in Poughkeepsie. That may seem strange for two guys getting ready to take one another's head off, but Ted and I respected each other and could separate our personal feelings and professional ambitions.

We trained at different times, but used the same sparring partners. For what it was worth, they predicted to me privately that I would knock Gullick out in the later rounds. But since they were Ted's friends, too, they probably told him not to worry about me.

Ten days before the fight, we moved back to Ohio to finish our training in Niles at the Eastwood Mall so the press could have a good look at us.

Ted chose to stay in Cleveland, while I stayed in Warren. That meant he had to drive 60 miles each way to training camp, which amounted to two hours a day in the car. That had to be a distraction, but not as much as Gullick's lady friend, who owned a tavern in Cleveland and was very attractive. The reports I got were that Ted was bouncing at the joint several nights a week, late into the evenings. The rest of the time, when he wasn't in his car and in Niles, he was with his girl-friend because he didn't trust her.

I believe the wrong type of woman has caused the demise of more boxers than all the other vices combined, because drugs or alcohol don't whisper bad career advice or mess up your legs. I was fortunate to have a woman like La Verne behind me as I prepared for the biggest fight of my career.

If Gullick's mind was on his lady more than on me, that was to my advantage. If he was sleeping with her up to the fight, he stood no chance. I've always been a firm believer in the old axiom that sex before a fight destroys a fighter. It takes at least 10 days to recover. I would abstain from sex for a minimum of six weeks before a fight—much to the dismay of La Verne. She sacrificed in more ways than one.

Coverage by the local news media of our training and fight was the best ever received for a Warren sports event outside of high school football. Writers and broadcasters from Warren, Niles, Youngstown, Akron, and Cleveland were prominent around ringside at the Music Hall.

One of the local reporters wrote that the winner of our fight would move up the ladder to bigger fights and more money, while the loser would gradually fade away from the boxing scene.

That forecast turned out to be right on the money. After our fight was over, one of us ascended to the heights of the boxing world, and the other dropped out of boxing, and ended up being killed.

CHAPTER EIGHT

Dirty Rotten Scoundrels

It took two years to get me and Ted Gullick in the ring. As it turned out, it was well worth the wait.

From the first bell, I took charge of the fight and established my superiority. I relied heavily on my jab and stung Gullick several times. During the in-fighting, I delivered damaging body blows. Gullick, meanwhile, tossed only a few punches.

I continued to pile up the points in the second round with my effective jabbing. Gullick appeared to be biding his time, but he did land two telling blows to my stomach and an occasional smash to my jaw, one of which shook me up pretty good. The latter punch seemed to invigorate Gullick, and the action was fierce from that point on.

In the third round, Ted landed another solid punch to my body. Then he cornered me and hurt me with lefts and rights to the head and body. I don't mind saying that the bell was a pretty welcome sound given the punishment I took in just three minutes.

In round five, Gullick turned up the heat and caught me with a vicious blow, but I shook off its effects and brought the crowd to its feet with a savage attack of my own to close out the round.

After some inconsequential sparring in the sixth, I uncorked a blistering right, followed by a swift combination and then a straight left to Ted's head. Down he went. Ted managed to make it up on one knee when referee Nat Brisken reached the count of 10 at 1:43 into the round. Now I was the heavyweight champion of two states.

I was 37-2, but I realized that most of my opposition had not been overwhelming. Nobody I'd fought had needed crutches to get into the ring, but there were a least a couple who could've used them—certainly afterwards. It was time to step up the class of my opposition. My wallet seconded the motion. Too many of my paydays had been worse than my opponents.

Two weeks later, in Beaumont, Texas, I blew Algie Waters out in two. George Foreman was at ringside. He was scheduled to box in Beaumont a few weeks later. Dean was trying to put together a match with Big George, who had built up an impressive unbeaten streak. But apparently Foreman's handlers didn't want his chin anywhere near me or my KO swings.

My reputation as a knockout artist didn't keep Charlie Polite out of the same ring as me, but it spurred the fighter who'd already faced Foreman and Frazier to take out a little insurance, first. Literally. Charlie wouldn't sign the fight contract until Dean promised to take out a life insurance policy to cover him in case anything happened during the bout. Charlie went out in three, but fortunately for him, it wasn't terminal.

The KO I scored two weeks later in Youngstown was nice, but the highlight of the evening was the presentation of the "Rocky Marciano Award" I received from the parents of the heavyweight champion who'd died two years before in a plane crash. The Marcianos were kind people, and we spoke at length after the match. They gave me a lot of praise and reminded me that Rocky had once hoped to sign me on as an amateur because of his fondness for punchers.

Awards were nice, but I was broke as a joke at this juncture in my career. With five mouths to feed, I actually considered chucking it all in for a decent paying 9-5 job with benefits. There were rumors about a fight with George Chuvalo for a decent payday, but you can't pay bills with rumors. To make things worse, the private war between Dean and Blackie had gone public. Their feud had spilled out into the local paper when Blackie declared that Chance owed him money.

Chance did receive most of the press where my management was concerned. He also was more involved in the day-to-day operations. Chance was more vocal to the press and was already a well-known sports personality. The press liked to quote him and photograph him. I believe all this made Blackie jealous. Gennaro handled the finances and Dean was the ring strategist. I tried to stay out of their feud, and just hoped that we could keep everything together and make us all some decent cash without too much more time passing.

That prospect got brighter when I signed to fight Vincente Rondon on August 26, 1972.

Rondon was the former light heavyweight champion from Venezuela, and his record of 37-7-1 and 20 KOs was impressive. He had lost his WBA title to Bob Foster the previous April and was now moving up to the heavyweight division. In his native country, Rondon had been awarded the title of "national sports hero," which he shared with Canonero II, a racehorse that had won the Kentucky Derby and the Preakness. It was a title well-deserved as he held wins over Jose Luis Garcia, and in his lighter days, Bennie Briscoe and Luis Rodriguez.

My friend Dave Matthews was my main sparring partner for the Rondon fight. I needed quality work with other talented heavyweights, but Blackie thought the added expense was a waste of money. Matthews always gave me credible work, but I needed to see a variety of styles to prepare myself for all contingencies.

Matthews had also sparred with Rondon and felt there was no way I could beat him because he had too much experience and ring savvy. Rondon had knocked Matthews down with 16-ounce gloves. He told me Rondon's punches were crisp and hard and could hurt me inside. I knew, however, I could hurt Rondon with one of my own crisp punches.

If I didn't stop Rondon within five rounds, Dave thought, I would be in real trouble. In our workouts he encouraged me to use combination punching instead of loading up on my right hand.

Rondon was 28 years old, and he was in the best shape of his career for our fight. He had sparred more than 100 rounds in preparation for his "now-or-never" battle against me. Saso Betancourt, Rondon's trainer, told the media that his fighter had been offered another big match in New York if he got by me, giving him added incentive to win.

But I wasn't without some advantages. One of them was my pal Ray Anderson, who had sparred with Muhammad Ali to help him get ready for Floyd Patterson. When we worked together, Ray taught me some valuable tricks of the trade. After Rondon arrived in Ohio for the fight, I watched him in a couple of workouts. He was pretty slick. He also gave his tongue a little exercise.

"Who has Shavers beaten?" Rondon asked condescendingly, adding that he hadn't come all the way from South America to lose. But I wasn't planning on losing, either.

Bo Belinsky, out of major league baseball now, had been upgraded from assistant cornerman to matchmaker for this event. He was also in charge of the ticket booth and was designated official training camp director. Dean loved to hand out titles to all of his friends.

Belinsky was having a difficult time adjusting to life without major league baseball, and Chance was trying to help him with an employment opportunity.

The Canton Memorial Auditorium was packed with a partisan crowd that expected me to give them something to cheer about. At the opening bell I immediately took the fight to Rondon.

In the second round, Rondon's nose started leaking blood.

I pretty much dominated the entire fight with the exception of the fourth, when Rondon got a little cagey. He managed to tie me up and get some good licks in. But overall, I was effective with both hands and hit him with everything but the ring post. Champion that he was, though, Rondon would not go down, and I couldn't keep my knockout string going. At least he could back up his tough talk.

The judges scored the fight 99-94, 100-90, and 99-94, all for me. It was the first time that I had gone 10 rounds. It was an important win for me, but other problems intruded on my celebration.

Pedro Tomez had refused to work in my corner because he wanted more money. I tried to explain to him that I wasn't making any money either. No one was. Even Dean and Blackie were still in the red. But Pedro wouldn't listen and walked away again. Chickie Ferraro of New York handled me in his absence.

I was back in the ring three weeks later against A.J. Staples, who I stopped in the first round.

Although my stock as an Ohio celebrity had risen with my recent victories, Dean still trumped me in that category, at least in some circles. One day Dean and I met at 11 a.m. in Akron at the gym. As we discussed our future boxing plans, an African-American man walked in and started toward us. Something about him gave me the creeps, and Dean had the same vibes. Dean whispered to me that we should leave. As we attempted to exit, the man started to ask questions about the gym. At the door, he suddenly pulled out a .38 pistol, and his hand was shaking. He had an itchy trigger finger. The creep pointed the gun in Dean's face and demanded his money. Chance froze.

"Give me all your money or I'll shoot!" the robber said. Then he dragged us into an empty storage room in the gym.

"Now empty your pockets!" he demanded to Dean. I had deposited a recent fight purse in the bank earlier that morning. I was dressed for a victory lap through town in a black pin-stripe suit. But the shabby gunman only had eyes for Dean. I thought about taking a punch at him, but I stood too far away to land a clean one and feared if I tried the gun could go off.

As instructed, Dean emptied his pockets and handed over nearly $500. We were then locked in the storage shed as the hoodlum made a clean getaway. Dean was dumbfounded.

"Earnie, why didn't he hold the gun on you?" he asked.

I replied as honestly as I could. "Dean, the brother knew when you are dressed the way I am, all my money is on my back and not in my pocket."

They never did get the guy who robbed Dean, but I had better luck against boxer Leroy Caldwell on October 25, 1972, in Newton Falls. My family and friends from high school were there to give me a hero's welcome as I stepped through the ropes at the high school gym. The Newton Falls Jaycees honored me earlier by proclaiming it "Earnie Shavers Day."

Caldwell was built like Hercules and had a 13-8-2 record since he started fighting in 1969. He had gone the distance with slugger Ron Lyle and had fought contender Cleveland "Big Cat" Williams. I stopped Caldwell in the second round.

My next scheduled bout never came off. I was supposed to fight Rico Brooks in Cleveland on November 29, 1972, but this time intimidation tactics went a bit far. Brooks had beaten Ron Stander, and Rico carried a 15-3-1 record into our proposed bout. He was the best available opponent we could sign.

At this point in my career, I was a little irritated by critics constantly questioning when would I eventually fight somebody with some ability. Well, I wouldn't be fighting Brooks either. After Brooks got off the scales at the weigh-in, I looked him up and down. I then took off my shirt, exposing 210 pounds of muscle while never taking my eyes off Brooks. That was the last I ever saw of the man. Brooks never made it to the arena that night. I have no idea where he hightailed it to, but if you're reading this, Rico, you can come out now.

The WBA, a major governing body in boxing, ranked me tenth in the world. I was scheduled to box Jimmy Young in Philadelphia next, and if I defeated him, a shot at former heavyweight champion Jimmy Ellis was on the horizon.

I trained on the West Coast with Willie Ketchum, and flew into Philadelphia 10 days before the fight. Then I trained at Joe Frazier's gym, located on Broad Street in a tough neighborhood a few blocks from Temple University and the Blue Horizon, which would become one of boxing's most well-known venues. The press gave me some great write-ups even though Young was the hometown boy.

A big benefit of training at Frazier's gym was that "Smokin'" Joe had the inside skinny on Young.

"Jimmy's a very slick boxer," Frazier said, "but he's afraid of your right hand. He's heard of your punching power." Frazier recommended that I set Young up in the first couple of rounds by not trying to knock him out.

"When you throw your right hand, don't throw it with full force until you are ready to turn the lights out on him," Frazier said.

The man knew what he was talking about. In the third round I knocked Young out with the right he feared so much.

Just minutes after the fight, the partnership between Blackie Gennaro and Dean Chance completely dissolved. Blackie had taken Dean to court over my contract. I was served legal papers by a private detective in my dressing room, and my purse had been attached.

The long-running dispute between the partners had come to a head with Blackie constantly complaining about finances and about Dean always stealing the headlines in the newspapers.

Blackie was green with envy, and told anyone who'd listen that the Gullick match was the only bout that showed a profit.

By the spring of 1973, the news of Blackie and Chance's breakup was common knowledge to boxing insiders.

I'll never forget the day La Verne and I were sitting in my mother-in-law's living room when we heard a loud knock at the door. I got up and walked over to answer it. I opened it and there stood a huge black man.

"Hello," said this stranger with an electrifying smile, and beautiful white teeth, holding out his big hand for me to shake.

"My name is Don King."

By the time I met King, he had been out of prison for over a year. He had been sent away for manslaughter after killing a man in Cleveland who owed him money for losing a bet in King's numbers operation.

King made the most of his time behind bars. He spent his days reading books on business, law, and philosophy. As he fondly says so often, "I didn't serve time, time served me."

King and Don Elbaum had co-promoted a boxing event together after King's release to benefit a near-bankrupt hospital in Cleveland with Muhammad Ali boxing in an exhibition. It was a success, and King was on his way.

Elbaum had been sold on King's charisma, and knew that King had the finances behind him from his numbers racket background. He told King that he could be the top promoter in boxing once Elbaum introduced him to the right people. The story goes that Elbaum told King that he wanted to introduce him to the fight people in New York and from there King would make the connections to eventually take over boxing.

"A black man will never be able to rule boxing," King said.

"What do you mean? This is America?" Elbaum argued. King shot back, "Yes, only in America!" Which is how King's signature catch-phrase originated.

King had tracked me down at my mother-in-law's house and invited himself in. It wasn't for tea and crumpets. He obviously had an agenda.

"I hear you're having some problems with your managers, Blackie Gennaro and Dean Chance," King said. "I would like to talk to you about your boxing career. May I come in?"

As he sat down on the couch in the living room, King said the word on the street had it that I was having problems with my two white managers. He put a special emphasis on the word "white."

King openly and shamelessly played the race card as a way of ingratiating himself with black boxers. The irony was that he loved having white heavyweights in his fighting stable. The only color that had King's stalwart allegiance was green.

He announced that he was there to buy out Chance's share of my contract, which was about 25 percent. Then he reached into his shoulder bag, took out $20,000 in cash, and threw it on the floor. The thud it made was followed by a deafening silence.

"I am not a broke nigger and I didn't come here begging," King said. That certainly got my attention. But he was merely showing, not giving. What he mostly did was talk. God, how that man talked.

La Verne was not impressed. As soon as King left, she warned me about the uneasy feeling that she had about our visitor. La Verne had always been quite perceptive. But we were short on money and King had a pipeline to big fights.

About a week later, King called to see if I wanted to go to Paris with him. He told me it would be a nice trip for us, mixing business with pleasure. The real purpose, of course, was to win me over to his side—and it worked. We were there for four days, visiting numerous museums and meeting prominent French businessmen. We even saw actor Omar Shariff gambling.

On the plane back, Don talked non-stop about how important he was and all the important people he knew. To this day, he's the only man I know who can talk non-stop over an entire ocean.

King picked up the whole tab for the trip, although I paid for it later, with interest. It wasn't hard to figure out King was a con man, but he was a con man with class and charisma. It was hard not to like the dirty rotten scoundrel.

I constantly had to remind myself when I shook his hand to look him straight in the eye, smile, and keep the other hand on my wallet.

CHAPTER NINE

Win, Lose, or Draw

King paid $8,000 for Dean Chance's share of my contract. Chance was a good friend, had a great boxing mind, and was a master promoter. He had strategically moved my career along, making me into a contender. It was sad to see him go, but when King bumped my salary up to $500 a week, I got over it.

I was the third member of King's stable. Working fast, he had already signed my friend Ray Anderson and heavyweight prospect Jeff Merritt to managerial contracts. Anderson had looked impressive as a sparring partner for Ali and "Smokin'" Joe Frazier, but he had constant problems with King. Ray was known for being difficult and had been dismissed from Frazier's camp after a dispute.

I took Anderson's dislike for King with a grain of salt, but within a brief amount of time I would come to understand that Ray's complaints had some merit. Anderson never got another title shot and eventually wound up as one of my sparring partners.

King suggested I move in with him at his farm in Windsor, Ohio, and train there. King was a breath of fresh air for me because with him in the driver's seat the bickering and back-stabbing over the direction of my career was finally over. Even though King was co-manager with Gennaro, he was running the show. King was the proverbial 800-pound gorilla, and of course, Gennaro wasn't long for his perch.

In the 1997 Home Box Office movie *Only in America*, based on Don King's life, there is a restaurant scene that shows King making a plea to take over my management duties from Don Elbaum. It wasn't even near the truth.

Through the years I have heard several rumors naming Elbaum as my one-time manager, and that is simply false. Elbaum did most of his promoting in the Cleveland area and was a bitter enemy of Dean Chance's. Once King took over my managerial duties, Elbaum may have advised Don or had an under-the-table agreement with him, but I never had a contract with Elbaum. In the movie I was quoted as saying, "Elbaum has been good to me." What planet did that happen on? It was Dean and Blackie who were my managers at the time King bought out Dean. Once King took over the reins, he went to work on moving my career beyond the borders of the Ohio state line.

King called Teddy Brenner, the matchmaker for Madison Square Garden in New York City, to arrange for a shot at Jerry Quarry. Brenner was intrigued by the proposition and asked King if I was training. King told him no because he wanted Quarry's people to think I wasn't in shape. In fact, I was training every day.

Brenner invited King, Gennaro, and me to fly into New York for a press conference to announce the fight for June 18, 1973. Everyone expected me to show up out of shape, and when we arrived at the Garden, they couldn't believe their eyes. Two days later we got the expected phone call from Brenner. He told King that Quarry had caught the flu bug while in training camp and had to pull out of the fight. Brenner said he was busy looking for a replacement. He called back the following day and asked if former heavyweight champion Jimmy Ellis was a suitable substitute for Quarry. No problem.

King brought in legendary boxer Archie Moore to start training me. The former light heavyweight champion who was boxing's all-time knockout artist arrived in Ohio a few days later.

Moore was an eccentric, but possessed one of the sharpest minds in boxing. He emphasized to us the importance of a boxer having a genuine training camp. Moore regaled us with stories of his own camp, the "Salt Mine," and how Cassius Clay—later Muhammad Ali—had once trained under him there. Moore said that is what gave Ali the idea of opening his own fight camp in Pennsylvania, and said Ali even decorated large boulders on the property with the names of former boxing greats, just as Moore had done at the Salt Mine.

King arranged with Ali for us to use his camp in Deer Lake. It was the most beautiful and well-organized training camp I had ever seen. Ali was very generous and gave us full run of his camp even though Ellis had been his friend since childhood.

After being in camp only a few days, King thought I needed a little free advertising. Soon a headline in one of the local papers blared, "Shavers Rocks Ali, Mild Riot Follows." In the story King was quoted as saying, "Earnie got thrown out of Muhammad Ali's training camp last Thursday because he hung one on the ex-champ's chin." The story went on to say that I had run all of the sparring partners out of the gym and that Ali had agreed to take up the slack and go five lazy rounds with me. When a reporter asked me if I put Ali on the canvas, I wouldn't lie, but I didn't tell them the truth, either.

"I ain't saying yes, and I ain't saying no," I told them. King also piously dodged a direct question from the reporter, stating, "Ali and Shavers have been lifelong friends; we will not say anything that will ruin that friendship." Even Ali's aide, Gene Kilroy, got into the act and called the incident a "mild riot" that lasted about 10 minutes. He said it started with our mouths, then got physical. The hell it did. It never happened.

King was always looking for that edge, be it in a marketing sense or in a business transaction. But the article had the desired effect—it brought me a lot of attention in the boxing world. The truth was, Ali and I never sparred. He did let me have free rein in his camp, but more important, he gave me advice on how to beat Jimmy Ellis. Ali and Ellis were from Louisville and there was definitely a rivalry between the two men.

The buzz the article created from King's imaginary Shavers-Ali fracas was about the most exciting thing that happened to me in camp. Mostly, it was strictly business. I did roadwork every morning and trained at 1 o'clock in the afternoon.

We had our own cook, although Archie often doubled as the house chef and prepared our meals. He usually served breakfast and called one meal the "Truck Driver Special." It consisted of three hamburger patties, four eggs, fried chicken, hash browns, four biscuits, and a secret, strange garlic drink.

Moore and I hit it off right away. I believe we got along so well because I didn't mind hard work, and I gave him 100 percent in the gym. He was from the no-nonsense old school. He let me know right away who was in charge and we didn't have any problems. He was there to teach. I was there to learn.

Moore often told me stories from his fight days and of his secret Australian Aborigine diet and the "goose juice" he discovered on a boxing campaign in South America. Archie was a con man at heart, and he and Don King often battled wits, trying to outdo each other. In this regard Moore was almost as slick as Don because he had been scammed countless times in his day. I respected Moore immensely because he had paid his dues several times over.

One of Archie's camp innovations was the "curse jar."

"Earnie, every time you, myself, or any of these guys curse, we have to put a dollar bill in. We can use the money to buy things for the camp," Moore said in all seriousness. He said it would also help improve our moral character in addition to helping the camp flourish. It was a win-win situation for everyone.

The way it worked was, the first time somebody swore it cost him a dollar. The second offense cost $2. The third time, $3, and so on down the line. A fight camp is not a seminary, and the pot got bigger as the days rolled on. Suddenly, when the jar was stuffed to the brim, we never saw it again.

"It's gone," was the only response I got from the tight-lipped ex-champ when I queried Archie about the mystery.

The way I looked at it, maybe Moore was just taking back what had been taken from him years before.

Having Ali himself at camp was another big advantage; he offered advice on how to fight Jimmy Ellis. The two grew up together in Louisville, Kentucky, and both were trained by Angelo Dundee. Ali knew every move Ellis ever made.

"You have to take the fight to Ellis and keep him from fighting his fight," Ali said. "He'll want to box you all night long."

Moore mapped out a fight plan designed to make Ellis try to out-punch me.

"Your job is to be in great fighting condition," he said. "My job is to create a strategy to beat Ellis. If you do what I tell you to do, you will beat him."

Moore had been after all the top fighters during his chase toward the championship title. He said all the big names ducked him for years, but he managed to always be in top shape in case he got lucky and got one of them to agree to give him a fight.

"You gotta be ready when your shot comes," Moore said.

One of the ways Archie got me ready was to have me chop a lot of wood.

"This will help tone your body and help you to increase your punching power," he said. He was right on the money—chopping firewood helped strengthen my wrists and gave me that extra snap when I delivered a punch. By my own estimate, I believe it increased my punching power by at least 25 percent.

Moore also counseled me on nutrition. For example, he told me never to eat frozen meat—it had to be fresh every day. Foods had to be prepared a certain way. On the day of the fight, he had me eat two steaks, but I was not to swallow the meat itself, just the juices. Moore believed the juices gave the body strength without taxing the body by requiring it to digest meat. The more energy the body saved, the more it could be drawn on in the later rounds of a fight.

Every morning Moore made sure I did my roadwork by 5 a.m., while the air was still fresh.

"The trees put out fresh oxygen early in the morning, which is what you want in your lungs," Moore instructed. When the cars and trucks got out during morning rush hour, Moore said, their cars emitted carbon monoxide, which wasn't good to breath into the lungs.

On days he had me scheduled for a full-tilt workout, he whipped up the "Truck Driver Special." Then I knew I was in for it later in the gym, and I would lose anywhere between eight and ten pounds by the time the workout was over.

The Old Mongoose taught me a lot about my own body and what to look out for. He warned me that if I could taste the salt in my own sweat, it was a plus.

Conversely, "If your sweat has no taste, it means you're stale from overtraining," Moore said.

Archie had me working on three different punches for the Ellis fight. They were the jab, the straight right hand, and the right uppercut. I worked on them so much they became totally automatic to me—just like breathing. When I saw an opening, I delivered the appropriate punch without even thinking.

Over the years the things Archie Moore taught me in 1973 have helped me time and time again. Moore was a very wise man and cunning as a fox. He was like a chess player when it came to mapping out a fight plan that included the psychological aspects.

"Start a sentence, but halfway through it stop and walk away," Moore advised me. "Whatever words come out of your mouth should work on your opponent's mind. Tell him something to agitate him or agonize over up to the time of the opening bell. It will hurt like a festering sore."

In Ellis' case I was to tell him he wasn't a puncher so that he would wear himself out trying to out-punch me. It's almost impossible to beat someone at what they specialize in; that's like someone trying to outbox Ali. What you do instead is make them fight your fight.

Once we arrived in New York, Archie went to watch Ellis train. As Ellis finished in the ring, Archie taunted him.

"James, you can't punch, so don't even try," Moore yelled at him.

The next day, with Moore again on the sidelines, Ellis was trying to show he could punch by beating up on his sparring partners. Some reporters remarked that it was highly irregular for a fighter of Ellis' caliber to be beating up on his sparring partners this close to a fight. Wonder who put that bug in the media's ear?

I trained at the famed Gleason's Gym in the Bronx. One of my sparring partners was Larry Holmes. He only had two professional fights at the time. I was told that his style was similar to Ellis'. Even as a novice professional, Holmes' left jab gave me problems. Larry showed a lot of potential that day, and it didn't take a genius to figure out he would go far in this business.

A press conference was held at a restaurant located near Madison Square Garden. Don King and I both attended. I was introduced first and briefly told the assembled press that I planned to defeat Ellis, thank you very much.

Then it was King's turn at the microphone.

Thirty minutes later King was still talking, and showed no signs of slowing down. He told the press that Quarry pulled out of the originally planned bout due to fear. He also stated that Ali had been offered $1 million to fight me for the title.

King then pointed to Angelo Dundee, who was standing in the back of the room.

"In the boxing world, Angelo Dundee is the epitome," King announced. Dundee wasn't impressed.

"Like hell I am," he said as he started to leave the room. "I'm Italian!"

When the press conference finally ended, King said that he had pictures available for the press. As the writers crowded around, expecting to be given a publicity shot of me, King instead handed out glossy 8x10 autographed photos of himself. It was a quite an unforgettable introduction to the New York press.

At the weigh-in, I tried a mind game of my own on Ellis. As he and Dundee were leaving the room, I instructed the security guard to go with Ellis.

"Make sure the oversized middleweight shows up for the fight tonight," I said loud enough for Ellis to hear. That remark had Ellis fuming. A minute later he bumped into Moore.

"Tell your boy I'm going to hurt him real bad," Ellis said to Moore with steam coming out of his nostrils. "I'm just telling you, Archie, because I don't want any blood on my hands."

"James, if you don't want any blood on your hands tonight," Moore answered without missing a beat, "don't wipe your face during the fight." Then he turned and walked away, whistling "Yankee Doodle Dandy." The Old Mongoose really knew how to take the piss out of a guy! I'm just glad he was in my corner.

Dundee was on to us. He knew we were trying to psych Ellis into thinking he could trade punches with me.

"Don't try and go toe-to-toe with Shavers," Dundee told him. "I want you to box." But Ellis would have none of that. His ego had been tweaked, and he was determined to prove to me that he could punch, too.

Early the next morning, Archie and I were downstairs in the hotel across from the Garden having breakfast. A few reporters came into the restaurant and spotted us. Archie saw them coming, so he took out a small brown bottle from his coat pocket and screwed off the top.

"Take a swallow and let out a roar, then stand up and roar again," Moore said under his breath.

I did as instructed and let out a roar the Lion King would be proud of. The papers reported that Moore gave me some secret potion from Australia. But it was simply a batch of cough syrup without a label. Who was sharper than Archie Moore?

The fight was really over before it even started. In round one, Ellis started off throwing combinations at me, but I bobbed and weaved to make him miss. He wanted to let me know how hard he could punch, but in doing so he made the mistake of leaving me an opening and I took it. Holding my right hand close to my side, I twisted my body in on upward motion and threw a devastating right uppercut. It landed on Ellis' chin and the fight was over.

"Earnie, that was the punch heard 'round the world for you," King told me that night.

The raves I got were nice, but my $60,000 purse would have been even nicer. I never saw a dime of it. Not one. I later found out that King had expensed everything to the point where there was no money to be made.

"Look, brother, I've never claimed to be a mathematician, but your math seems a little fuzzy," I said to King. "Where did the rest of the money go?"

"Expenses ate it all up, brother," King said with a shrug and a sheepish grin. When I called him on it, he already had the paperwork ready to back up his figures.

"I sent my grandma to Europe, so you're going to pay for that. And my grandkids need to go to college, so you're going to pay for that, too. The wife needs a new fur coat, so you're going to have to pay for that too, champ," he said.

I put a lot of King's kids through school.

Not surprisingly, Blackie Gennaro was also having financial difficulties with King. Sly dog that he was, King would double-bill everything. King was the master of manipulation and knew how to make the balance ledgers say whatever he wanted. King confused poor Gennaro with his slick and unscrupulous accounting methods. For example, King would come to Blackie with a bill for $20,000 and ask him for half. Gennaro would cough up $10,000, not knowing that was the actual whole amount of the bill. King always double-billed Gennaro on everything and patted him on the back at the same time.

I was taken by King many times. As a token of their appreciation, King and Gennaro bought me a brand-new 1974 Lincoln Continental Mark IV, which cost about $13,500. Gennaro gave his half to me. King's half came to $7,000. King paid for the car, but he took it out of my fight purse. Although the vehicle was a gift, King got his money back tenfold. If I didn't miss any payments, the car would be paid off in 20 years!

After some time back in Ohio with the family, it was back to business. I returned to training for the Jerry Quarry fight which had been rescheduled for July 25, 1973, at Madison Square Garden.

We set up our training camp at Grossinger's in upstate New York, with Archie Moore again at the helm. Because of my first-round knockout of Ellis, the Quarry fight meant more ballyhoo and a lot more money than I was used to. I was promised $40,000, against 27½ percent of the gate.

At Grossinger's I was sparring with Jeff Merritt, a dangerous puncher like myself. Merritt had it in for me because of some past sparring sessions we had after he was released from prison. I had gotten the best of him every time. To put it kindly, Big Jeff was a loose cannon.

Jeff thought Don showed favoritism toward me, and we had nearly come to blows over a meaningless card game a few weeks earlier. Larry Holmes was also playing. There was a few grand on the table and I had the winning hand. Merritt claimed it was a misdeal because of some exposed cards. I grabbed the money off the table and invited Merritt to fight me over the cash. He knew better. I rarely got upset, but when I did, I meant it.

Merritt was the only boxer available to work with, which was too bad because he clocked me with a left hook when my mouth was open and broke my jaw. The Quarry fight was off once again.

I flew home the next day with my jaw wired shut. The fight was rescheduled for later in December.

In the meantime, Archie Moore was fired because Teddy Brenner wasn't happy about what happened with Merritt. The Garden had spent a lot of money promoting the fight and somebody had to answer for it. It couldn't be me or Don King, so they chose Moore as the scapegoat. I was sorry to see him go; he was a great trainer and fight strategist. He commanded respect and demanded a 100 percent effort. I missed him, and it would show in my performance against Quarry.

King replaced Moore with a friend of his—Tiger Brown from Cleveland. Brown was an okay trainer, but he wasn't world-class like Archie. I didn't have peace of mind with Brown like I had with Moore, who knew the sweet science inside and out. Brown was a decent enough guy, but as a trainer, he belonged in the amateurs. Anything Moore told me was religion.

On top of missing Archie, right up to fight time King and Gennaro were arguing again and trying to get me to take sides. On the very day of the fight itself, when I should have been thinking only about Quarry, I was inundated with phone calls at all hours from both of them trying to win me over.

Quarry was riding a four-bout win streak coming into our crossroads fight. He had twice lost to Muhammad Ali and had been stopped a few years earlier by Joe Frazier for the world title. But after hiring Gil Clancy as a trainer, Quarry worked his way back into the heavyweight picture, and was ranked fourth going into our bout. I was ranked sixth.

The oddsmakers had Quarry as an 11-to-5 betting favorite because he had more experience against better quality opponents. Quarry's record was 47-6-2, with 28 of his wins by knockout. I had 34 consecutive victories, 33 by knockout, and wasn't lacking for confidence, at least, in print.

"Quarry loses to fighters above a certain level," I told *New York Times* sportswriter Dave Anderson. "I'm above that level." But come the night of the fight, I was below sea level.

Shortly after the bell, Quarry came rushing at me and gave me a pummeling like I'd never experienced before. He beat me like a bass drum for two minutes without any sort of retaliation on my part. Seconds later, I toppled backwards onto the canvas, my right glove holding one of the ropes. I felt as if I were holding on for dear life. However, I got up quickly.

Moments later, Quarry continued his ravaging assault, and at 2:21 of the first round, referee Arthur Mercante signaled the end of the scheduled 12-round bout.

It was a bitter lesson in the harsh reality of boxing. Six months earlier, after I stopped Jimmy Ellis in the first round, I had so many friends and fans in my dressing room, even I couldn't get in. Fast forward to after the Quarry fight, when I was in my dressing room all alone. Even my shadow was hiding under the table. It reminded me of one of Don Kings sayings.

"I'm with you all the way, win or draw," King said. "But lose, and you're on your own, baby."

CHAPTER 10

World War III

It's been said that King dropped me like a hot rock after the Quarry bout. Not so. He advised me to take some time off to spend with my family.

Four months after the Quarry bout, Gennaro sued King in Ohio District Court for non-payment of monies due him from the Ellis and Quarry fights. In August, the lawsuit was settled, King paid Gennaro an undisclosed sum, and Blackie ended up in the driver's seat. I didn't fight again until May 16, when I scored a first-round knockout over Cookie Wallace.

My career had been at a standstill when King bought out Dean Chance and the doors started to open wide for me. King had the connections that led me to my biggest fights at that stage of my career, even though he didn't pay me for them.

I know it's controversial to say, and it may even be outrageous to some, but I count Don King as a friend. King is a businessman first and foremost. The money he never paid for the Quarry and Ellis fights I eventually did receive years later through an employment opportunity set up through Don's wife, Henrietta King.

I was disappointed when King was no longer in charge of making my fight arrangements. I wasn't thrilled to have "El Cheapo" Gennaro running things because I knew I wouldn't get any financial support. At least King had paid me a $500 weekly salary. With Gennaro I received a weekly salary for doing cement work for his company. Let's put it this way: Gennaro and I barely tolerated each other on a personal level. One day, while driving heavy equipment for him, I found out how he really felt about me.

That day, my 1962 GM station wagon was giving me problems and I pulled into a gas station. One of my co-workers was also there with a big pickup truck with a cab in the back. I asked for a lift to work and jumped in the back of the cab. When we got there, I decided to stay in the back of the cab to play a prank on Gennaro.

But the surprise was on me.

Gennaro pulled up a few minutes later, fuming. He didn't see me in the back and inquired as to my whereabouts by asking, "Is the nigger here?"

The guys in the front seat tried to signal him with their eyes that I was in the back of the cab. Gennaro didn't catch their cue and said, "Are you having eye trouble? Where's that nigger Shavers?"

"Yassuh, boss, right here," I said, popping up out of the backseat like a wind up jack-in-the-box. Gennaro's eyes got big as saucers and he looked like he had just seen a ghost. Fumbling for words, he pointed to his sun-tanned skin and tried this beauty.

"Uh, look Earnie, I'm darker than you," Gennaro said.

"Oh, not quite," I said. "Right now, I'd better see some green!" Then he went into his pocket and started pulling out a wad of hundred dollar bills.

"Keep counting," I said patiently. "I can be bought. Now buy me!" He must have apologized for the next six months.

In November, I lost a 10-round decision to Bob Stallings, a slick New York fighter. I felt rusty after the long layoff. I was 30 years old and felt my career was heading nowhere.

Three weeks later I took a rematch with Jimmy Young. I was confident that I'd score another knockout victory over him. I took him lightly and paid for it. Young had improved as a boxer and he surprised me with his new skills. The fight went the 10-round distance and was called a draw.

At this point in my life I was becoming fed up with boxing. I even considered throwing in the towel. I packed all my stuff from camp into my old station wagon. On my return home, I told La Verne that I was done with boxing. La Verne commented that all I needed was a mule, because I looked like a gold prospector the way my vehicle held everything I owned.

I felt like a prospector who had been on the road for years but had only claimed a few nuggets of fool's gold.

I figured La Verne would be relieved when I told her that I was finished with boxing. I was wrong. After I unloaded the car she tossed all my gear right back and told me, "You've come too far to chuck it all away because you're frustrated right now."

Her support made me realize I wanted to give boxing one last try.

After January 1, 1975, I started to train again. My first fight for that year was February 11, in Orlando. I stopped journeyman Leon Shaw in the first round.

I collected two more victories and then signed to fight contender Ron Lyle in his hometown of Denver, Colorado. Lyle had spent seven years in the Colorado State Penitentiary for second-degree murder before capturing the national AAU heavyweight championship in 1970.

He was backed by cable television founder Bill Daniels, who also owned the Utah Stars of the American Basketball Association. Daniels had seen Lyle spar in prison and guided him to an unsuccessful shot at the heavyweight crown against Muhammad Ali on May 16, 1975.

Four months after being stopped by Ali in the eleventh round of a fight the judges had him winning, Lyle chose me as his first comeback opponent. I left for Denver 10 days before the fight to adjust to the altitude of the Mile High City.

Frank Luca, my new head trainer, told me I had to knock out Lyle because I wouldn't get a decision in his hometown. Luca was a friend of Gennaro's and had some knowledge of boxing. But he was chosen as my trainer not because of his boxing know-how, but because he came cheap.

This was a crossroads bout for both of us. Lyle was making his first appearance back home in 14 months. He had suffered a devastating loss to Jimmy Young three months before losing to Ali. I was now ranked seventh in the world, and the winner of our clash was promised a shot at Foreman. Guess who George must have been rooting for?

At the weigh-in, Lyle shadowboxed as I climbed on the scale.

"You're going to have to do more than that tomorrow night," I said confidently as he threw light punches in the air.

"All this talking is going to have to come to a halt," Lyle replied. "Now you're gonna have to fight. I'm gonna bust your tail. How many times you been down?" Lyle was referring to my loss to Jerry Quarry, I guess. Lyle himself had never kissed the canvas, but I promised him that was about to change. It was a promise I kept.

The Denver fans backed their fighter. When Lyle entered the ring, the place exploded. I had entered the lion's den.

During the first round, Lyle and I moved and boxed. I paced myself until the fireworks started exploding a round later.

I hit Lyle with a left hook that sent him down, hard, and apparently out. The fight should have ended right then, but the referee took his time escorting me to a neutral corner and then started his own count over Lyle instead of picking up the official count of the timekeeper, who was already up to seven. With the ref's help, Lyle had plenty of time to clear the cobwebs, and then the bell sounded ending the round. Lyle would later say that the knockdown punch I landed was so hard that it untied his shoelaces.

After Lyle was saved by the bell he got another huge break. The customary 60-second respite was somehow stretched to two minutes, giving the local hero additional recovery time, and by the time round three ended, Lyle was himself again. Eventually I punched myself out, and the match was stopped in the sixth.

I voiced my opinion the next morning to the *Denver Post*. The Colorado Boxing Commission had stolen the fight. I said I had been warned about the commission before the fight, and, sure enough, I had gotten a royal screwing. I won the fight in the second round, but not surprisingly, nobody wanted to hear it. I didn't really figure it would go any differently, but I wanted my side to be in the record. Eventually I cooled off, but I never fought in Colorado again.

I soon had something to cheer about when La Verne gave birth to our fifth and final daughter, Amy, on October 13, 1975. Now when I fought, I could look forward to an all-female rooting section.

On November 26, I finished the year by knocking out Tommy Howard in the third round in Monroeville, Pennsylvania.

I hadn't intended that to be my final fight of 1975, but opponents kept canceling out on me. Five fights went by the boards that way. I needed to create some attention for myself, and then I remembered something Archie Moore told me.

"Earnie, you are the best puncher that I have ever seen," Moore said. "You must come up with a plan to get into the money." My plan was to come out with a brand-new Earnie Shavers, at least in appearance. I needed a look fans would remember, and the place to start was my head. I shaved off all my hair, and then completed the new look by adding a mustache and removing my smile. This gave me the menacing appearance that fans remembered. I looked like a Mongolian warrior. As Don King's light-socket hairstyle was his trademark, my bald head and cold stare became mine.

More importantly, the phone began to ring again.

I got a call from Don King's office offering me a March 28 fight with Kevin Isaac, a tough fighter from Brooklyn. A few years earlier, Isaac gave Larry Holmes the first knockdown of his career, and I'm sure he was going to try to give me all I could handle. Two days later, Teddy Brenner called to offer me a fight that same day against Henry Clark in Paris. Clark was a fringe contender for years and defeated respectable opposition like Mac Foster. However, Clark wasn't the puncher Isaac was, and the purse offer was much more to my liking.

I had already signed Don's contract and sent it back to him. King's fight would pay me $5,000. Brenner offered me $20,000 to fight Clark, which was a much easier fight for me. I'm not a mathematician by any stretch of the imagination, but it wasn't hard to figure out which one was the better deal.

King once told me that every contract had a loophole in it somewhere; you could find it if you looked hard enough. So I pored over my contract with him for the Isaac fight, studying it until something hit me. King had misspelled my name. In his contract, my first name was down as "Ernie."

You see, $5,000 then was just like $5 million to me now. I had five fights in a row fall through on me, and bill collectors were taking a number at my front door. When the contract came from Madison Square Garden for $20,000, I just asked myself, "What would Don do?" Hell, I took the $20,000 fight.

King went to court to try to stop me, of course. When I heard about the lawsuit, I sent the judge a fax with the correct spelling of my name. At the hearing, the judge asked King if he had a contract with me. King said yes, and when the judge asked to see it King handed it over. The judge took a look at it and said, "Mr. King, your contract spells Mr. Shavers' first name E-R-N-I-E. The correct spelling of Mr. Shavers' first name is E-A-R-N-I-E. Next case, please."

King actually looked at me as if he were proud of me. It was all a game to him, and I just happened to win this one.

The Henry Clark fight was televised live on NBC. Clark bore a slight physical resemblance to Muhammad Ali, but it ended there. This was the right fight for me at this time. I flew over to France with La Verne, Frank Luca and his wife, Theresa, and my sparring partner, Ray Anderson.

At Clark's final public workout, I stood there, bald and beautiful, never taking my eyes off him, watching him everywhere he went. I had a cold, mean look on my face. When he finished working out, I walked over to him for a few words.

"I came here to die and I'm taking someone with me," I said with gritted teeth. Then I turned and walked away. That put the fear of God into him.

I had a badly bruised right hand, and so I had to rely heavily on my left jab come fight time. That was enough for a unanimous decision victory. The day after the fight, Clark confessed to me in the hotel lobby that I had scared the shit out of him with that shtick on his last day of training.

Six months later, we met again underneath the last bout of the Muhammad Ali-Ken Norton trilogy in New York's Yankee Stadium on September 29, 1976. Ours was the bout preceding the championship fight, but the real story that night was the atmosphere surrounding the fight.

For reasons I still haven't figured out to this day, the entire New York Police Department decided to call for a strike. That was all fine and dandy; our boys in blue could always use a good raise. However, they chose, of all places, the Ali-Norton fight as a forum to air their dirty laundry to the media.

Preceding the fight, the police came out with pickets, shouted at the top of their lungs, blew whistles, banged on drums, and blocked traffic in front of Yankee Stadium. Even worse, crimes were being committed in front of them and they chose not to lift a finger. Not exactly model behavior from the guys who keep our country from total anarchy.

Even Ali was not immune to the ruckus. His limousine was blocked from entering the grounds, with a rowdy mob jumping up and down on his front fender and rear hood. Ali, a pied piper of crowd control, didn't dare get out of the safe confines of his limousine. It took his driver a good amount of time to inch his way into Yankee Stadium 45 minutes before his fight started. I'm sure that played on Ali's mind, and his head wasn't where it should have been.

The mob, seeing nobody was going to write them a ticket if they got out of line, took free rein over the fight. They rioted, looted cars, slashed tires, pick-pocketed fight spectators, and wreaked havoc on everyone.

More than 10,000 of New York's finest thugs scaled the walls of Yankee Stadium to see a free heavyweight title fight in person and thumb their nose at authority at the same time.

We were apprised of the situation in the dressing room, and were told to leave all of our valuables inside our lockers. Welcome to the Big Apple.

If the situation in the stands was scary, I found no reason to be scared when I got into the ring. This time my right mitt was mended and raring to go. Clark went out in two.

Ali's night was much tougher. He went a full 15 rounds and was named the winner over Norton by a controversial decision. The verdict was loudly booed by the large crowd, and was the subject of intense media debate.

I saw Ali at the post-fight press conference. We had remained friends since he had given me access to his training camp. But I wanted a shot at his title. Ali told the press he would fight me if I defeated his former sparring partner, Roy "Tiger" Williams.

Ali thought it would never happen. Ali and Williams had a disagreement in camp and every day their workouts turned into World War III. Williams was 6'5" tall and weighed 240 pounds. He could punch and he never smiled. After just a couple of days of giving Ali all he could handle in the ring, Williams was let go.

Williams was familiar to me. I remember hearing of him when I turned professional and was training in Poughkeepsie. A Philadelphia fighter at camp named Lloyd Nelson warned me about this hellacious puncher, and said if I ever fought Williams I should make it worth my while.

"Get all the money that you can get for the fight, because it's going to be a life-and-death fight for both of you guys," Nelson said.

When I was training for Ron Lyle, we had brought Williams in as a sparring partner. Every session was a toe-to-toe workout, a complete gym war. After about a week. Frank Luca put an end to it.

"These kind of workouts are no good, Earnie," Luca said. "You leave all the fight in the gym. We'll have to let Williams go."

I put my hands together, looked up to heaven, and said, "Thank you, Lord! You just saved me from having this guy shot in his sleep."

We only agreed to fight Williams became if I got past him an Ali fight would ultimately mean total financial security for me and my family. I wasn't thrilled to be facing Williams, and I knew going in that it would be the toughest test of my career. We fought in Las Vegas on December 11, 1976.

It turned into a hellacious struggle. The first eight rounds I stayed close, hitting him in the body and wearing him down; but I took my own share of leather in return. I was ahead by a slight margin going into the ninth. Then things got real dicey.

Sensing he was behind, Williams picked up the tempo. Two hard right hands sent me staggering across the ring. I tried to punch back, but I was too tired to return fire. Williams spun me into a corner and banged away with left hooks. I tried to tie him up to catch a breather. Finally the bell rang. Only one round to go with this monster, and now it was anybody's fight.

Luca told me I had to win the last round convincingly. Williams came out bombing again in the tenth. He backed me into the ropes and let both hands fly. I was in a sitting position on the ropes and wasn't firing back. The referee jumped in and administered a standing eight count.

When the action resumed, Williams moved in for the kill, but I caught him with a right hand and sent him staggering.

I pinned Tiger against the ropes and kept punching until the referee stepped in to give Williams his own eight count. I could hear my corner screaming "twenty seconds!" I was fatigued and even that seemed like a lifetime.

As the referee finished his count, Williams staggered sideways and fell to the canvas. The fight was ended at 2:46 of the final round. When I watch that bout on tape, I still get the willies.

After a few weeks' vacation with La Verne and the girls, I was back in training camp in Las Vegas preparing for Howard Smith, a former sparring partner of mine and a stablemate of Ken Norton. My Ali fight was still in the negotiation stage, and I was offered a decent payday to fight Smith on national TV.

The training went well, but two days before the fight I came down with the flu. I might have pulled out against anybody else, but I knew Howard Smith pretty well. Earlier that year I stopped him every day in the gym with the big 16-ounce gloves on.

The only one who knew I was sick was Frank Luca. We never even told Gennaro. As we were leaving the weigh-in, I ran right into Smith and his trainer, Bill Slayton. I decided to use some of the psychological strategy Archie Moore taught me.

"Hey, Howard. Remember the old days?" I said with a sly smile, then a wink. I wanted Smith to think about the times he quit in our sparring sessions.

I was going out of the door when I heard Howard say to Bill Slayton, "I'm not ready for him." Flu or no flu, I knew I would beat him because he was afraid of me. I stopped him in the second round, chipping a bone in his neck and retiring him.

Life going into the Ali bout couldn't have been better. La Verne and our daughters now resided in a colonial 10-room house that sat on 100 acres six miles outside of Warren, Ohio. In my spare time I tended to the garden, fished, listened to jazz music, and watched my favorite television series, *Kojak*.

I was excited about receiving my shot at the title, but I considered Ali a friend. I never forgot his generosity in allowing me to use his training camp free of charge and for the advice he had given me on past opponents. But this was my shot at boxing immortality; all other considerations went on the back burner.

It was time to prove that I was as good as the best of them, and even better than the "Greatest."

CHAPTER ELEVEN

Ali and Me

The experts claimed that I was catching the 35-year-old Ali on the downside, and that an upset was possible. Not only was Ali advancing in years, boxing was only one of the activities on the champ's busy agenda.

In the months prior to our September 29, 1977, world title bout at Madison Square Garden, Ali had gotten married again on June 19, 1977, to Veronica Porche.

Earlier that year, I fell for a Veronica of my own. I was introduced to Veronica Taylor through a mutual friend. Veronica was a nurse in Youngstown and she was gorgeous. Her beauty took me by surprise, and the funny thing is that she looked very much like Ali's new wife. They could have easily passed for sisters.

My Veronica had been married once before and had a son. She was in no hurry to rush back to the altar, which made it easier for both of us, since I already had a wife. Veronica never asked me for anything or put pressure on me to see her all the time. She left her schedule wide open in order to be available for me. She realized I needed to spend time with my children and I had to be totally focused on boxing.

While adding a mistress to my already busy schedule didn't make life any less hectic, it did force me to become more organized in time management. Years later, it would cost me dearly in alimony.

Over the years, the celebrity I gained from boxing brought me in contact with many extremely attractive ladies. Being the red-blooded, all-American male that I am, I sometimes succumbed to the temptation of their charms. They were more than I could resist, although I confess that, unlike between the ropes, in this case I didn't always put up my hardest fight.

Looking back, I think La Verne knew about my attraction to other women from the start, but she never said anything. La Verne was the best wife and mother anyone could ask for. I should have never gotten involved with another woman, and it was the worst move I ever made. In addition to having two women, a still-wandering eye, and a houseful of children, I also had Ali on my plate.

Still, when it came to serving yourself in the buffet line of life, I had a ways to go to catch up with the self-described Greatest of All Time. A movie about Ali's life story, naturally entitled *The Greatest*, had just been released with Ali starring as himself. Ali's commercial ventures also continued to multiply. He even lent his name to a pesticide manufacturer for a household roach killer. Muhammad was a busy man, and if defending his world title wasn't his top priority, his health and championship were in jeopardy against me.

Some members of the press theorized that Ali should quit while on top instead of risking it all against a deadly puncher. But Ali would have none of it. He enjoyed the limelight too much and wasn't ready to step out of it. He even went so far as to bait me in my own hometown newspaper, the *Warren Tribune*:

> I'M HIS IDOL—his family, his children, they all like me. He likes me, too. He admires me.
>
> He came on the bus after Quarry knocked him out in one round. Wanted to know if I'd give him a little advice. He didn't forget all that. He's getting into the ring with his MASTER! With his LORD OF THE RING! And now, he's meeting the PROFESSOR of boxing! HE'S MEETING ME!
>
> And now, he's got all the pressure of the crowd, and the championship, and the bell ringing, cameras and flashes.
>
> You all understand—this gets to a man. It ain't just who hits the hardest. It's a good mind game. In the gym, he fights a better fight than he will the night of the championship match.

BUT KNOW, he's fighting Muhammad Ali. THE LIVING
LEGEND! He's fighting the most recognized face in the
WORLD!

It didn't bother me. Ali was just building the gate for the
fight. It was what some reporters wrote that smarted. After the
Lyle and Quarry defeats, my courage was questioned. Many in
the press still knocked my stamina, calling me a five-round
fighter at best and saying that I was easy pickings for anybody
who took me beyond that. I reported to training camp early for
the Ali bout determined to silence my critics.

Frank Luca and I agreed that the summer heat in Ohio
would adversely affect my training. People always talk about
our cold winters, but the summertime can be pretty brutal,
too. I knew that in the extreme heat my weight would drop too
fast and I would end up too light for my world title challenge.
What I actually needed to do was put on some weight.

I usually liked to train for nine weeks for any big fight,
and they didn't get any bigger than fighting Muhammad Ali.
Unless I put on at least 10 solid pounds, I feared I would come
in too small for the fight. Frank and I decided to go into camp
two weeks earlier than usual to do some extra muscle-building
work. We started on July 7 at Turkana Farms in Calcutta,
Ohio. The contract called for me to get $25,000 for training
expenses. But since Blackie's friend owned the camp, we got
the place for free. That was classic Blackie—always cutting
corners on expenses. Even in a major bout like this, old habits
die hard and Blackie couldn't overcome his thrifty ways.

The first 10 days of camp were dedicated to tree chopping
and boat rowing on a private lake near the camp. It was good,
hard work designed to build up my arms, shoulders, and back,
and therefore put even more heft into my punches. But after
all that and my daily roadwork, sparring, and everything
else, I still ended up eating a lot of ice cream to pack on the
additional weight.

About 10 days before the fight, we headed to New York to
finish up there and help with the media buildup. A week later,
La Verne and the girls came out. I hired a chauffeur-driven
limousine to show them the city. It was a good feeling to have
my family close by for the most important event in my career.

I also maintained contact with Veronica back in Youngstown. I knew it was wrong, but I was unable to call off the affair. Her sex appeal had won me over and I couldn't help myself.

Rumors surfaced that Ali had been knocked down twice while sparring with Jimmy Ellis, the same guy I had KO'd in less than a round. Was it truth or just hype? Nobody knew for sure, but to play it safe, the New York State Boxing Commission made Ali submit to an electrocardiogram.

At the pre-fight press conference Ali tried to get into my head with his usual carnival spiel, but it didn't work. I knew him too well, and we were friends. When the press wasn't around Ali would carry on a normal, civil conversation with me. Once the media was present, Ali would go instantly into his act.

And what would a Muhammad Ali fight be without some kind of demeaning nickname for his opponent? Sonny Liston was the "Big Ugly Bear." Floyd Patterson was the "Rabbit," and George Chuvalo was the "Washer Woman." My nickname was kinder and gentler. Ali dubbed me the "Acorn" because of my shapely bald noggin.

It didn't bother me. I just reminded everyone that from acorns grow mighty oaks. I think my good-natured demeanor was well received by the media, but it didn't inspire a lot of belief in my ability to take away Ali's title.

The media asked how I would counter the "rope-a-dope" strategy that Ali successfully used to regain the heavyweight throne against George Foreman.

"If he starts to rope-a-dope, it's gonna be the dullest fight in history," I replied. "When he starts with the rope-a-dope, I'll just hit him a couple of times and then go over and lean on another rope and stare at him. It will be a staring contest."

Then I overheard Bundini Brown, leaning toward Ali, saying, "Hey, champ, I think it's going to be a long, long night." I looked at both of them and just nodded my head, as if to say, "You got that right, Bundini." I had trained like a madman, sparring 215 rounds for the fight. I was in the best shape of my life.

At the physicals the day before the fight, Ali was up to his old, shopworn antics. I arrived first, and after jumping through the required medical hoops, I made a beeline for my locker room. I knew Ali was on his way and I was in no mood for his games. When Ali arrived and was told that I had already gone to my quarters, he came over and started banging on my locker room door. I could hear him putting on his squirrelly show, yelling for the Acorn and the usual nonsense.

I couldn't help but laugh. Almost every fighter fell into Ali's trap, either getting genuinely upset or trying to match his shtick—a losing proposition either way. But I just sat tight until Ali left, and my refusal to play the straight man in his charades badly frustrated Muhammad. I could sense his disappointment through the door before he gave up.

Of course, Ali told reporters that it was a mental victory for him. By the sound of it, Ali had gathered a large press contingent on his side of the dressing room door, and made the most of it by feeding them a monologue.

"He [Shavers] didn't want to see me today," Ali told the reporters. "Tomorrow night when the national anthem is being sung and the crowd shouts 'Ali! Ali!', he'll live a whole lifetime. He'll say, 'I must be crazy. How did I get myself into this mess?'"

Our fight was the first world heavyweight title bout at Madison Square Garden since March 8, 1971, when Ali met Joe Frazier in their first historic match for the undisputed title.

This was the 19th title defense for Ali in two separate championship reigns, and the 22nd championship bout of his career.

I had won 52 of my 54 fights by knockout, giving me the best KO percentage (.963) in boxing history. That was higher than other famed bombers such as George Foreman, Joe Frazier; Rocky Marciano, and Joe Louis.

The night of the fight I left early for the Garden. There I noticed that a television set had been placed in our dressing room. Neither Blackie, Frank, nor I gave it much thought at the time, but it turned out to be the most important television in my life, but I didn't know it until after the fight.

NBC was broadcasting the fight live, and as an extra attraction the network arranged to flash the officials' scorecards on the screen after every round. The implications were not lost on Angelo Dundee, Ali's veteran trainer. He posted matchmaker Eddie Hrica in Ali's dressing room to watch the TV set there and relay the numbers back to Ali s corner after each round.

In my dressing room, I laid on a table to relax. Before I actually dozed off I thought about the bus loads of fans making the eight-hour trip from Warren. Since the fight was on a Thursday night, many of my blue-collar supporters had taken off that day and planned to sleep on the bus going back to Warren following the fight and punch-in for work on Friday. Ohio had not had a world heavyweight champion since Ezzard Charles in 1951, and my friends and fans were willing to lose a little shut-eye for the privilege of telling their grandkids that they were there when the Acorn flattened the Butterfly.

I slept right up to the time of the fight when I was awakened in a way my sainted mother never used when I was a boy.

"Earnie, it's time to get ready and for you to go out and kick some black ass," Frank said.

I got up, got dressed and had my hands wrapped. Then I loosened up. Surprisingly, I felt very relaxed; in fact, maybe too much so, considering the occasion. But Frank had me adequately psyched up. He kept asking me the same question: "What is going to happen to Ali s entourage after you win this fight?" Then he answered his own question: "They'll all be over here looking for the employment office."

I had it all worked out in case they came looking around my house. "I'm going home to put up a picket fence around the house, get some guard dogs and put my wife, La Verne, at the door. They may get over the fence, they might con my dogs, but they will never get past La Verne. She's in charge of my entourage."

As the challenger, I entered the ring first. With Blackie and Frank following closely behind, we jogged to the ring with the theme from "The Mod Squad" blasting throughout the sound system in the Garden. Every fiber in my body tingled as I made my way to the ring.

Welcome to the big time.

After I climbed through the ropes, the spotlight flickered as Ali started on his way to the ring. The greatest showman in boxing whipped the crowd into a frenzy, and it seemed like everyone in the Garden but me was screaming his name. All that fanfare did not fool nor scare me. I knew the real Ali. I remembered back to the time I had spent with Muhammad.

In those days, I got a chance to know a kind and gentle man who had hopes and fears just like my own. A man who I could talk with—at least until there was an audience. For Ali just had to play to the crowd, that was his life. He loved to be the center of attention. Now he was about to get some serious attention from me in the ring.

In all the time I trained at Ali's Pennsylvania camp, we never sparred with each other. Ali would come in and watch me against the other guys, see me stagger them, and then quietly say afterwards to anyone around, "I can take him, right?"

I used the memory of his obvious uncertainty to motivate me now.

It was somehow fitting that the first time we entered a ring together it was to be for the ultimate sporting prize, the heavyweight championship of the world. It was the precious moment I had been waiting for since I started boxing, the reason for all the blood, sweat, and tears I had shed.

I never felt better in my life. At his age, it was unlikely, it seemed to me, that Ali would be up to 45 minutes of moving around the ring at the pace required to keep me off him. I was two years younger, and I had not been in as many wars or taken as many punches as the legend in the other corner.

Even as the referee called us to ring center for his instructions, Ali couldn't keep himself from clowning. He put his right glove over my head and attempted to give me a shine. I wished I had a dime on me at that moment so I could give him a tip.

The bell finally rang and Ali began as he said he would: flat on his feet, circling to my right but not dancing, easily eluding the few thunderbolts I launched. He didn't so much win the opening round as I gave it away.

Midway through the second round I unloaded a thunderous right hand over Ali's left jab, which caught him flush on the head. Hurt badly, Ali clinched and held on for dear life. But over my shoulder he made faces at the crowd to give the impression to everyone—and especially the voting officials— that he was spoofing. I stepped back and hesitated, watching Ali put on a rubber-legged act that was closer to the truth than he wanted me to know. It was an Oscar-worthy performance that made even me wonder.

My instincts told me I had the champ reeling, but I let Ali con me into thinking otherwise. If, at that crucial moment, I had taken the fight to him, the title could have changed hands right there. But Ali's recuperative powers were extraordinary, and he recovered quickly. His antics bought him the time he needed to clear his head.

After that the pace slowed, and the third and fourth rounds were a seminar in defense conducted by both of us.

"Come on, Earnie, throw some punches, the crowd is watching you, this is your night," Ali taunted.

"They're watching you, too, you throw some," I replied. When he even tried to goad me into throwing something for him to counter by calling me a nigger, I retaliated in kind.

It had been ingrained in me since day one in training that I shouldn't punch myself out, that I should take it easy early on. My handlers figured that Ali would try to draw me in, then sit back and absorb my punches until I burned myself out.

Looking back, it was a crazy strategy. I was never going to lay back and out-point Ali. I remembered Ali being so cunning in the second round when he was hurt. I didn't want to go in for the kill and get killed instead. Ali was the kind of guy who, when you thought you had him hurt, always had the ability to come back. He always seemed to pull off miracle after miracle.

If only I had not held back in that second round, and instead had thrown everything I had. I might have won the title right then. But I didn't and what turned out to be my biggest window of opportunity was slammed shut.

Ali had said before the fight that he was one to gamble with fate, to dare to dare, and laugh in the face of danger. He played a shrewd but dangerous role, surviving on guile and guts. He was a master of deception who covered his diminished skills with a magic show.

My battle plan was to be patient, not to be a wild man and not to punch myself out. It may have caused me the championship. In fact, I know it did.

During the first seven rounds, Ali mostly played. He talked and posed and threw a limited number of punches. He played peek-a-boo along the ropes and often grabbed them and held when I pushed my attack. As promised, I retreated back to ring center when this occurred.

The crowd voiced its disapproval of Ali's tactics by booing in the eighth round. He yelled right back at them. Referee Johnny LoBianco complained to Ali's corner about his lack of effort at round's end.

Going into the ninth, we figured the fight was close. But Ali's comer didn't have to guess, thanks to the runner who was relaying the officials' tallies broadcast on the TV in the champ's dressing room. To this day I kick myself thinking about the tube in my dressing room, sitting there unused.

In the ninth I picked up my attack and rocked Ali with a few right hands. Ali decided to return fire and then some in round 10. He fired numerous combinations in a concerted effort to end the contest then and there. He never staggered me, but he clearly took the round.

Now I was entering uncharted waters. I had never boxed more than 10 rounds, and now the endurance that so many questioned in me would really be put to the test. I wasn't exhausted, but in the eleventh round I showed my first hint of fatigue by stumbling after missing Ali with some Hail Mary shots.

Round twelve was close, but I took the next two rounds by constantly pressuring and out-punching Ali. In the 14th, Ali hit the canvas but it was ruled a slip.

Coming out for the final round I felt I had a good chance to pull out the decision. I was ready to let it all hang out. There was still plenty of dynamite left in my punches to knock him out. All I needed was an open shot.

At the end of the 14th round, I had sensed Ali was fatiguing. It seemed to take a mammoth effort for him just to get back to his corner. He slumped down on his stool, his eyes glazed with weariness. But then he found out something I didn't know. Dundee's runner brought back the intelligence that the officials' scorecards had Ali in front, and all he had to do to seal the decision was stay upright for the final three minutes.

When the last round started, Ali sucked in a deep breath, lifted himself off his stool, and came out dancing. I went right at him, throwing everything I had left.

I missed with a big right hand. I took two of Ali's punches, and missed with another powerful right, followed by a left hook, and then landed a right. Ali was weary, but he dipped into his reserve tank and flurried right back.

We both lurched around the ring, swinging, missing, gasping. With less than a minute to go, Ali called once again on his tremendous will power to launch perhaps his greatest offensive of the evening. As Dundee watched in amazement from his corner, he could not believe what his eyes were seeing.

"I don't know how you do it, you son of a bitch," he later told Ali, "but I love you for it."

I was momentarily stunned by the champ's sudden storm, but I sucked it up as well and tried to punch back. When the bell sounded, I thought I'd done enough damage to pull out a close decision.

The voting officials didn't see it that way.

Judges Eva Shain and Tony Castellano each tabbed Ali the winner, 9 rounds to 6. Referee Lo Bianco scored it for Ali 9 rounds to 5 with one round scored even.

In his dressing room, the thoroughly exhausted winner-and-still-champion told the media, "That Shavers is sure one tough nut to crack. He hit me so hard he shook my kinfolk back in Africa."

While Dundee was hailed as a genius for keeping abreast of the televised scoring, our failure to take advantage of the same opportunity by leaving the set in my dressing room unattended all night gave new meaning to the term "boob tube." Luca told the press he was afraid he would overreact if he knew the official score. But at the same time, Frank lent an uncritical ear to the between-round evaluations of several members of the Ohio Boxing Commission, two reporters, and Jose Suliaman, president of the World Boxing Council.

All were unofficially scoring the fight and all reported regularly to Frank that they had me far in the lead. Unfortunately, they were keeping score with their hearts and not their heads.

"No sweat," they said, "don't take any chances, Earnie." You didn't beat Ali unless you knocked him out.

It was nice to read in the next day's *New York Times* that legendary sports columnist Red Smith pegged me a slight winner (the *Times'* boxing beat reporter scored the fight a draw). But after reviewing a tape of the fight several times, I couldn't argue with the decision. Ali won the fight because you have to take the title away from the champ, and I didn't.

It was a pretty costly victory for Ali. Afterwards, people openly called for his retirement. Matchmaker Teddy Brenner of Madison Square Garden went so far as to declare that Ali was not welcome to fight there anymore because he didn't want any part of such a risky venture for the champ.

After the fight, the New York Boxing Commission had a full medical done on Ali. They gave Ali's physician, Ferdie Pacheco, a laboratory report indicating that Ali's kidneys had suffered severe damage. Pacheco went to Ali and pleaded with him that the time had come to call it quits immediately and to retire to the good life. But Ali didn't listen, and Pacheco stepped down as his doctor rather than be a party to the disaster he was sure would result from Ali's continuation on the firing line. Muhammad could not see into the future, he could not contemplate the terrible damage he was doing to himself. If only he were not so damn brave.

The record book says that I lost to Ali, but that's not the whole story. I ended up on the wrong side of the decision, but I walked out of the ring with a moral victory—the most important kind of all. It was said that I had a punch, but nothing else. So what? All heavyweights are supposed to be able to punch. They also wrote that I could not take a punch and had a glass jaw. But what hurt most was when reporters wrote that I lacked heart. It takes heart just to climb through the ropes. What the hell did they know about heart from behind a typewriter?

Now people treated me differently. The Ali fight proved that I wasn't a dog and that I wasn't afraid to go 15 rounds. As the great Cus D'Amato told me, "Earnie, tonight you became a man."

My high school senior photo.

Standing with the finest woman I ever knew: my mother.

In happier times with my first wife La Verne.

*One of my last photos with a full head of hair.
I would soon shave my head for a Mongolian warrior
look. I wanted a gimmick that matched my punch.*

Holding the hand mitts for my close friend Kenny Rainford.

I liked to find diversions to relieve pre-fight stress. Here, I'm fishing in upstate New York before my second fight with Larry Holmes.

Clowning with Jimmy Ellis who went out in the first round once the 10-ounce gloves were put on.

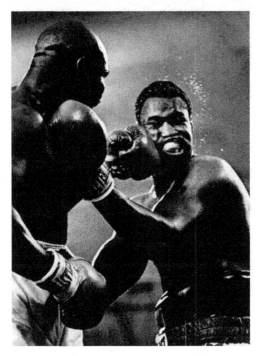

Duking it out for the world title against "The Easton Assassin" Larry Holmes.

I land a hard right to an overly confident Muhammad Ali during our championship bout in Madison Square Garden on September 29, 1977.

Down goes Holmes! But unfortunately not quite long enough. I'm still not sure how the champ beat the count after eating my right hand.

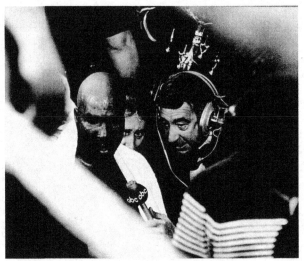

*Reviewing a replay of the fight with
the legendary Howard Cosell.*

In a matter of seconds it would be lights out for Ken Norton.

Posing for photos with my good friend
"The Greatest" Muhammad Ali.

Me and former light heavyweight champion Michael Spinks.

This was the only time George Foreman and I were ever in the same ring. Michael Carbajal looks on.

It's "Hawk Time!" with former junior welterweight champion Aaron Pryor at the Boxing Hall of Fame in Canastota, New York. Sadly, "The Hawk" passed in 2016.

*At the Boxing Hall of Fame induction cere-
mony with Grand Marshal Al Lewis ("Grandpa
Munster") and James "Bonecrusher" Smith.*

*Me and George Chuvalo, another
1970s heavyweight contender.*

Me and Sugar Ray Leonard. We fought on the same bill on September 28, 1979, in Las Vegas.

In London with former light heavyweight champion John Conteh and actor Denzel Washington for the premiere showing of "The Hurricane."

At the National Boxing Hall of Fame Awards in Southern California with my good friend Kenny Rainford. Kenny presented to me my award as I was inducted into the Hall in 2017.

Sports agent Martin Gover, me, Mike Tyson, and fight referee Richard Steele in attendance at Mike's one-man show "Undisputed Truth" in Las Vegas.

Me and my beautiful wife, Rita, attending a 2017 fundraiser in Las Vegas for John Walsh to raise money for missing and exploited children.

At New York City's Madison Square Garden, in July 2017, revisiting where Ali and I fought 40 years earlier.

CHAPTER TWELVE

All the Marbles

For the Ali bout I received $300,000, the biggest payday of my career. It didn't compare to Ali's $3 million, but I was happy.

I celebrated by flying the family first class to London for an unforgettable 10-day vacation. The girls always had a tutor when we traveled so they would not get behind in their schooling. That was a must for me, them completing their school work.

We went to see a couple of plays while we were there, but the girls' favorite form of entertainment was watching the changing of the guard at Buckingham Palace. They also really enjoyed meeting some pen pals they had been put in touch with by a neighbor. It became a ritual for the family to embark on an annual road trip.

The pain of defeat wore off pretty quickly. The Ali fight opened a lot of doors for me. Even in England I was recognized frequently. More than 70 million people had viewed the fight worldwide.

When I returned home, the phone wouldn't stop ringing. There were proposals for fights, speaking engagements, and interviews. *Boxing Illustrated* released its list of annual awards soon after the fight and named me its "Inspirational Fighter" of 1977. The Ali-Shavers match was designated "Fight of the Year."

The Good Housekeeping Seal of Approval was still a long way off, however. When I returned from England, I spent as much time with Veronica as I could manage. I knew it was wrong, but I was in love. The affair never interfered with my family life. The money I spent on Veronica was money I'd have spent on myself anyway. She never put a bit of pressure on me. Looking back, I think La Verne knew about it from the beginning or at least had her suspicions. But I had a good family life and didn't want that jeopardized. I was a two-woman man for the next several years.

After five months off, I signed to fight unbeaten heavyweight contender Larry Holmes. But I only had four weeks to prepare for our March 28, 1978, bout at Caesars Palace in Las Vegas, because Blackie wouldn't let me go into training until the contracts were official. He was afraid he was going to be out a few dollars for training expenses if the fight didn't come off.

Don King was back in my life, but this time only as a promoter. I knew better than to ever consider another management contract with him unless I was a glutton for punishment. King sold the fight to ABC-TV for prime-time showing. ABC contracted to pay me $325,000 and Holmes $200,000. It was billed as a World Boxing Council (WBC) title elimination bout, with the winner to get a shot at Leon Spinks' heavyweight title, which he'd won from Ali a month before. I was the number-two contender and Holmes was number three. Spinks subsequently got stripped of the WBC belt for signing for a rematch with Ali, and the WBC named Ken Norton its heavyweight champion.

I knew that Holmes was going to be very tough. I remembered back to the sparring session we had in New York when Larry only had two professional bouts. His spear-like jab and fluid movement had given me problems then. No doubt he had only improved with time. So cutting off the ring was bound to be a problem.

Larry's is one of the true rags-to-riches stories in boxing. Holmes dropped out of school in eighth grade and worked for minimum wage at a car wash. Boxing was his only hope out of a life of poverty. He had been a decent amateur boxer but turned pro in 1973 with little fanfare in Scranton, Pennsylvania.

Richie Giachetti, a Cleveland trainer and associate of Don King, had seen my sparring session with Holmes at Gleason's Gym in New York. It was the eagle eye of Giachetti that had convinced Don to take Holmes in hand.

At the time, Larry was 24 years old and making peanuts on the Scranton club circuit. Within just a few weeks, King lined up a bout for Larry in Madison Square Garden and purchased him a brand-new satin robe with the nickname "Easton Assassin" embroidered on the back. King made Larry feel like he was going places.

But it wasn't long before King began to feel differently. When Larry fought undefeated prospect Kevin Isaac in his third bout under King, he showed guts by coming off the floor to stop Isaac in the third round. But that knockdown bothered King, who started paying more attention to his other prospects.

In his biography of King, *Only In America*, author Jack Newfield recounts what happened to Holmes on the undercard of a Roberto Duran fight in San Juan, Puerto Rico. Larry was fighting tough Billy Joiner of Cincinnati for a mere $1,000 purse. Don asked Larry to carry Joiner for a few rounds to kill time before the scheduled televised appearance of Duran, but Holmes stopped Joiner in three. Since their agreement was only verbal, the aggravated King tried to get away with paying Larry only $300. Only after an enraged Holmes threatened to punch King out did Don cough up the other $700.

Just a year earlier, in 1977, promoter Bob Arum, King's arch-enemy, tried to lure Larry away from Don by offering him more than $50,000 to face Young Sanford, who Holmes had already agreed to fight for King for $10,000. When Larry tried to get out of the King deal, Don threatened to have his legs broken. Larry took the threat seriously enough to purchase a .22 caliber gun. For the next month Larry carried the weapon wherever he went, even during his morning roadwork.

For all his mistreatment at the hands of King, Larry realized he was too close to a title shot to change horses. He was unbeaten in 26 fights, and a victory over me would propel him into the high-rent neighborhood of the heavyweight division.

Frank Luca had studied several videotapes of Holmes' fights. I watched a few, too, but spent a lot more time in the gym than watching the VCR. At age 33, I wasn't sure how many more battles my body had left. In training I left nothing to chance. At Johnny Tocco's Ringside Gym in Vegas, I sparred 245 rounds for Holmes, 30 more than I had for the Ali fight.

I worked on rolling my body to the left and right and throwing hooks with both hands. My plan was to attack Holmes' midsection throughout the scheduled 12-rounder.

But there were problems aplenty in camp, most of them caused by Blackie's tightfistedness. My purse for the Holmes bout was $300,000, but only $5,000 had been budgeted for training expenses. Blackie wouldn't even heat the place where I trained when I wasn't using Tocco's. It played on my mind. Blackie took nearly 50 percent of my fight purse, but I was given the training allowance of a four-round preliminary kid. Once again, Blackie refused to pay for top-notch sparring partners. It went from ridiculous to almost comical when Blackie would challenge the price of a meal that I ordered off a menu. If I ordered a $5 lunch, he argued that the $4 daily special would be just as good. Blackie nickel-and-dimed me to death on every expense. The feud between us almost reached the boiling point several times during training, but I tried to focus on the job at hand.

I knew Holmes would be determined to prove wrong those who called him just a cheap imitation of Ali, with his fast hands, dancing feet, and running mouth. He had defeated some tough opposition, like Roy "Tiger" Williams, on his way up. Larry had broken his right hand in the Williams bout and had primarily been a one-handed fighter ever since. His tonsils still worked just fine.

"I haven't even said hello to a girl in the last 30 days," he told the press before our match. "For me, that is a world record. After all that, if Shavers thinks I'm gonna run from him, he is nuts. I'm going to be on him like white on rice. He says that anybody who stands up to him gets knocked out. We're gonna find out."

That was encouraging. If he meant it—which was doubtful—at least we wouldn't be putting on a track meet instead of a fight.

Legendary boxing trainers Ray Arcel and Freddy Brown were brought in to prepare Holmes for the biggest fight of his career. Between them, Arcel and Brown had trained 39 world champions, including Ezzard Charles, Kid Galivan, Tony Zale, and Roberto Duran. That was a whale of a lot of experience in one comer.

Holmes' educated left hand gave me trouble from the opening bell. Larry moved around the ring and popped out that rapid left jab for the entire round. Sometimes he doubled and even tripled up on it. I was a little tense trying to work my way inside, bobbing and trying to slip that metronomic jab. It came faster than any jab I had ever experienced. I even started blinking in anticipation of it.

The second round produced some interesting moments. In the beginning Holmes was moving and jabbing. When he moved in close for a brief exchange, I heard a distinct tearing sound. I didn't know what to make of it. As the round progressed, I was able to land a decent right hand to Larry's head. It was the kind of punch I would need to land often to win the bout. Holmes stepped back and shook his head, an indication of the blow's effect. He answered back with a left and a right cross.

At the bell, the mystery of the weird tearing sound was solved. As I went to the corner for the 60-second rest period, I turned for a glance at Holmes and got a shock. The moon was shining brightly! Larry had split his boxing trunks.

It didn't keep him from dancing for the next two rounds. With that ramrod left, he kept me from reaching him with a clean shot. I was off balance and frustrated—and then I was bleeding, to boot. That damned jab cut me high on my cheek bone.

Between the third and fourth rounds, Larry got a change of drawers. His shorts had kept splitting worse, and his guys literally cut them off in the comer and pulled on a replacement set of trunks.

I was winning the fashion show, but the fight was a different story. Holmes kept moving side-to-side, creating angles that made it difficult for me to hit him. I pinned him in a corner in the sixth, but he fired back and moved out of harm's way. In clinches, I tried to push Larry off balance in order to land a clean shot, but he rarely let me get that close to him. The next several rounds followed the same pattern.

In the 12th round, Larry connected with a solid right hand that buckled my knees. He followed up with a big combination right before the bell. When it rang, I knew I had lost. The judges confirmed it. Harold Buck and Joe Swessel gave Larry every round, scoring it 120-108. On Dave Moretti's card (119-109) I was given round 10, but that was it.

I offered no excuses. It just wasn't my day. I had tensed up early and never really found my groove. I had tried too hard to land the one-punch bomb to end it, and got caught by too many of Holmes' shots.

Months later, Holmes took a close decision in a thrilling contest over Norton for the WBC title. With that pistol-like jab, I knew Larry would be around for a while. As for me, after back-to-back losses to Ali and Holmes, I was now standing in the back of the line. But I still had my power, and I wasn't ready to hang up the gloves yet. I was more than ready to call it quits with Blackie, however. I'd had enough of his relentless hassles about money, which had made our training camps pitched battles over expense accounts. Somehow I always ended up on the short end, as was the case in the Ali fight.

"Look, Blackie, we were given $25,000 for expense money," I reminded him. "You only spent $8,000 on training. Where's the rest of the money?" He offered some lame excuse that didn't amount to a hill of beans.

Eventually our attorneys got involved. The four of us sat down one day at Blackie's home to sort things out. After I excused myself to go to the bathroom, I overheard Blackie and his lawyer attempt to strike a deal with my attorney to buy him off. That was it as far as I was concerned. When I came back, I said, "Look, Blackie, you're doing some funny things with my money. I want my contract back."

A buy-out would cost me $200,000, Blackie said.

"I will not pay you $200,000 for my contract," I told him. "I will pay you $50,000, $25,000 on the upcoming Norton fight and another $25,000 for the Larry Holmes fight. After that, that's it." Then I got up and slammed my fist on the table.

I wasn't done, though. If he didn't take my offer, I said, my next step would be to go straight to the Internal Revenue Service and sing like a canary about the unusual business practices of one Joseph "Blackie" Gennaro.

"And then somebody's going to be in some mighty big trouble," I said with a caustic tone. In case he wasn't buying it, I threw down an envelope addressed to the IRS I'd taken the time to prepare earlier. At that point my attorney jumped up and broke into the conversation.

"Earnie, I think you're acting rather hastily...."

"Shut up!" I cut him off. "Don't say another word." Then I turned back to my manager and said, "Blackie, I want this to be a closed case today."

"Oh, OK," said Blackie, looking a little wilted. "But promise me you won't report me to the IRS," he pleaded.

"We'll see," I said, and then I walked out of his house. In the next day or so, Blackie's lawyer drew up the agreement and the issue was resolved. I was now not only the world's hardest-hitting heavyweight contender, but his manager, too.

I retained Frank Luca as my trainer. I told Frank that he could represent himself as my manager to the media if he wanted, but that I was the one calling the shots. I'd pay him 15 percent instead of the usual 10 percent fee to book my fights, but all deals were subject to my approval, and only my signature on a contract would count.

Like many in boxing, Frank had a case of sticky fingers. I knew that going into our new arrangement, but was willing to live with a little larceny as long as Luca didn't get any Willie Sutton-like delusions of grandeur.

A sure tip-off that he was overreaching was when Frank would preface a proposal by telling me, "Earnie, have I got a deal for you!" What that meant was that it was an even better deal for Frank. If he'd tell me, for instance, that he'd gotten me "X" amount of money to fight Larry Holmes, the first thing I'd do was go over the contract myself. Fighters weren't supposed to do that. It was taken for granted that we were too dumb to understand, if we could even read it in the first place.

After I checked the fine print, I'd tell Luca, "I want five first-class tickets, four rooms, and another $50,000, and then we've got a deal." Frank was counting on pocketing about $50,000 for himself, so I cut out $50,000, and let him keep $10,000. See, I didn't mind if he made a little money for himself, everybody did that. He could steal $10,000, but no way was he going to steal any more than that.

"I'll go back to them and see what I can get," Frank would say, a hang-dog look on his face. But I already knew what the deal was, and when Luca came back with everything in order, I'd say, "Hey, Frank, I was born on a Friday night, not last night. Got any more sweet deals for me?" I knew he couldn't say no to what I'd laid out because then he'd lose the $10,000 I'd let him have. I didn't mind getting screwed, but I did mind getting royally screwed.

Years later, Luca's questionable ethics put him in the "big house" for eight years when he used his position as a church official to bilk investors in Nevada and Arizona out of $11.4 million.

Luca eventually pleaded guilty in September 1997 to using a pyramid scheme to get investors to give him money for bogus real estate developments, in which he cheated roughly 300 investors. I guess you could say I was lucky he liked me.

It wasn't just the boxing end of things I kept an eye on. I planned to do a few television commercials for a clothing store in Las Vegas, which was arranged through Dean Chance. I also did some spots for Pony sportswear, which signed me to a nice deal.

ABC-TV enticed me to be a participant in its *Superstars* program which involved well-known professional athletes and celebrities competing against each other in a series of fish-out-of-water events like tennis, swimming, weight lifting, bicycling, golf, track, bowling, row-boating, and the infamous obstacle course that was always the grand finale to each show.

The show's headquarters was the Princess Hotel in the beautiful setting of Grand Bahama Island off the coast of Florida. It was an enchanting place with sandy beaches, crystal blue waters, and year-round sunshine. It was a chance to get away from the rigors of the gym and relax and pick up a nice piece of change, too.

I was invited to compete against other world-class athletes, which included basketball stars Maurice Lucas, George Gervin, Kevin Grevey, Doug Collins, and Gail Goodrich. Hockey stars included Bryan Trottier, Yvan Cournoyer, Mario Tremblay, and Wayne Cashman. Rounding out the roster were fellow heavyweight contender Jimmy Young, ice skater Toller Granston, soccer goalie Shep Messing, and water ski jumper Wayne Grimditch.

The way the show worked was that each contestant had to pick 7 out of 10 events to compete in, not including his specialty. The winner of each event was awarded 10 points, and so on down the line. Each point was also worth $100, and the top three performers got bonus money, the first-place winner pocketing a cool $10,000, second-place $5,000, and the third-place finisher $2,500.

The highlight of the show for me was when I took top honors in the 100-yard dash, with a 10:64 time. No one from the show knew I ran track in high school, and I genuinely shocked the hosts, football golden boy Frank Gifford and basketball legend Bill Russell.

"What a surprise by Earnie Shavers!" Gifford said as he witnessed a 215-pound boxer leave the rest of the athletes in the dust. Russell noted that I wasn't going to break any world records, but said I had good technique.

My technique in swimming, however, needed definite improvement, as I took dead last in that event and had to dog-paddle the rest of the way in to make sure I didn't drown. Overall, I placed somewhere in the middle of the pack, but the best place for me to show off my wares was still in the ring.

Four months after losing to Holmes, I took a tune-up bout in Virginia Beach, Virginia, against journeyman Harry Terrell on July 20, 1978. I hadn't won a match in over a year and was looking for a confidence builder. The 10-4 Terrell fit the bill nicely. I had him down twice in the first round. Harry barely beat the count the second time, near the end of the round. Things weren't getting any better for him in the second, and Terrell decided there was no point in going any further.

After padding my new winning streak with two more no-sweat KOs, it was time to get back into the high-stakes heavyweight sweepstakes. Before my recent tune-up victories, I had signed to fight Ken Norton, who was no chicken dinner. In fact, I was expecting him to be a full seven-course meal with all the fixings.

CHAPTER THIRTEEN

Ray of Hope

I was now 34 years old, and former WBC heavyweight champion Ken Norton was somewhere around there. More secretive about his real age than a Hollywood starlet, Ken had been listed as 32 for several years running, and I wondered if Norton himself even knew for sure how many candles to put on his birthday cake.

One thing was for sure: the bout against Norton was a must-win for me if I wanted to get within punching range of the title again. When I went into training in January 1979, the Ohio weather was freezing. I didn't want to take any chances of coming down with the flu, so Frank Luca and I decided to set up our camp in Las Vegas, where the fight would take place.

Without Blackie Gennaro around pinching every penny until Lincoln yelped in pain, it was the best training camp I ever had. My friend Ash Resnick at the Aladdin Hotel handled everything. He set us up in a beautiful home on the Sands Golf Course and arranged for our own private gym in a warehouse away from the Strip. We usually trained at Johnny Tocco's gym, but this time we wanted the privacy to work on a few things and also afford me the most peace of mind as I prepared for the fight that would make or break me.

The Norton fight would be a broadcast on ABC-TV. It was a package deal, with Larry Holmes defending his WBC title against Puerto Rico's Ossie Ocasio, upset winner over Jimmy Young, the winner to meet the Shavers-Norton winner.

Appearing on the undercard was my former sparring partner, Akron, Ohio, native Michael Dokes. An amateur sensation, Dokes was 11-0 in the pros and was being groomed by Don

King for heavyweight stardom, and eventually he did briefly hold the WBA version of the title. I had sparred with Dokes in Ohio. He was a gifted fighter with great speed and threw wonderful combinations. But Dokes had an insatiable taste for the wild life, especially drugs. My warnings about such things fell on deaf ears, as did cautions about keeping an eye on the people who were supposed to be keeping an eye out for him. Don King, for instance. I explained to Dokes about some of King's ways and how he needed to safeguard himself, but I should have kept my mouth closed. Dokes made a beeline straight for King and told him everything I said. A preening peacock who handed long-stemmed roses to women at ringside before his bouts, Dokes must have been a stool pigeon in a previous life.

Speaking of birds, Gennaro would've had one had he been around to see us spend $40,000 on training expenses for the Norton bout. I was only getting paid $100,000 in all. Three-to-one favorite Norton was in for $750,000. The huge purse disparity didn't upset me. When I was done, Ken's take would start a nice retirement fund for him.

I was in my best condition since the Ali fight. I trained down to 210 pounds, and I hadn't felt as good in years. It showed in my sparring. One partner insisted on wearing a ski jacket in the ring with me because I was punching so hard to the body.

While we practiced our real strategy for the fight in private, Luca and I presented different versions to the media. I told them I was going out to hit Kenny on the jaw, and Frank said to the body. I said he would last three rounds, and Luca told reporters Norton wouldn't make it through the second. Then we looked at each other and laughed, knowing neither was the real plan we had in mind. We were so full of shit, but we had a fight to sell.

Six weeks before the bout, I laid the psychological groundwork for Norton's demise at a press conference hosted by Don King. King was calling the card "Star Wars," but he made it clear at the press conference that he considered Holmes and Norton the shiniest members of the heavyweight galaxy.

Don went so far as to start hyping a future rematch between them as if Ocasio and I were mere sitting ducks for them. Ocasio may well have been that for Larry, but I decided to let Norton know that looking past me would be an even worse career move than those cheesy *Mandingo* films he made in the mid-1970s. When I spoke up, King brought me to the podium. On my way past Norton, I looked him in the eye and said "Kenny, I'm going to destroy you!"

Norton had once been offered $1 million to fight me, and he turned it down flat. That was a lot of dough for just one fight. The only reason he had agreed to now was to get another shot at Holmes. I could tell how much he was dreading it by his response to my in-his-face declaration at the press conference. Instead of puffing up those "Mr. Universe" pecs and rising to the bait, Norton just sat there impassively and mentioned that we would both make a lot of money.

"Yes, but I'm going to be the only one to remember that," I said forbiddingly. Norton looked like he was already doing his best to forget that and everything else about our fight.

I was confident, all right, but I couldn't take Norton too lightly, because he was still a major force in the heavyweight ranks. He held an official win over Ali and had lost two very debatable decisions to him. The decision against him in the Holmes fight could have just as easily gone to Norton without causing boxing fans to reach for their Maalox.

My plan was to go right to Norton, back him up and make him fight. Kenny kept his back leg locked in the ring, which made it awkward for him to fight while backing up. Our plan— the real one—was to make him back up and to pin him against the ropes and let the punches rip.

We knew that Norton's trainer, Bill Slayton, wanted Norton to try to force me into the later rounds to tire me out. But instead of running me around the ring, their strategy was to fight me inside in hopes of nullifying my punching power. Little did they know that that was exactly where I wanted Norton, too.

My only concern was about Norton getting the decision if the fight went the distance, but I didn't lose much sleep over that prospect because I intended to make it a short fight for both of us. I knew I was ready, and as frank taped my hands in the dressing room of the Hilton Hotel, I was so relaxed I was almost falling asleep.

"You all right, Earnie?" Frank asked. "You're looking so cool and calm." That was correct. I had paid my dues in training camp, and my mind was totally at ease. Everything was coming together perfectly and I knew that I was going to win. It's a marvelous feeling you only get a few times in your career—that absolute confidence in winning. I had it that night.

It wasn't necessary, but seconds before the opening bell Luca gave me his best "Win one for the Gipper" speech.

"Remember all the babies we gotta feed!" Luca yelled. He was referring to my six daughters and his four children. If you can't inspire your boxer any other way, go right for the pocketbook. Works almost every time.

One look at Ken shuffling out toward me told me he was afraid—and a bad dancer. The only dancing Norton ever did was in a disco, and even Frankenstein had more jive in his step than Kenny. He had never been fast, but now Norton was slower than I had ever seen him before. He was an easy target.

Taking a page right out of our playbook, he elected to lay against the ropes and catch my punches and counter-punch. When that didn't work, Norton decided to just cover up and let me punch myself out. Incredible mistake on his part. This side of beef stood a better chance against Rocky Balboa.

Any part of Norton's upper body left unprotected by his curious peek-a-boo defense, I blasted. Ken lowered his head, tucking his chin on top of his right wrist. His right glove was laid against his left cheek—a virtual invitation to whack him with a left hook, which I gladly accepted.

In the very first minute, I hit Norton with a wicked hook to the liver and then another to the head. The latter was a bomb that exploded on his temple. Norton didn't go down, but all his circuits were scrambling.

The next punch was a left hook that caught Norton flush on the head. A right nailed him as he was going down. He rolled over and managed to regain his feet by the count of eight, but then staggered back against the ropes and nearly fell again.

After referee Mills Lane decided the fight could continue, I decided otherwise. I hooked Norton to the head and then a right uppercut sent him tumbling down again. The former WBC champion crawled to the ropes on instinct alone and even pulled himself up, but Bill Slayton leapt up the steps to save him from further punishment. It was over at 1:18 of the first round, and I was the top contender again. It was my 55th knockout victory in 65 fights, and my 20th first-round knock-out. And now I was going to fight for the title against Larry Holmes, who had no trouble that night against Ossie Ocasio.

But first Holmes was obligated to defend against lightly regarded challenger Mike Weaver on June 22, 1979, at Madison Square Garden in New York.

Had it been a physique contest instead of a fight, Weaver, a body beautiful called "Hercules," would've been the odds-on favorite to win. But in the ring his impressive muscles were of very limited value, and at 20-8, Weaver was seen as such a non-entity that the TV networks declined the opportunity to broadcast the fight. Home Box Office, then a fledging affiliated cable TV system reaching two million homes, paid $200,000 for the broadcast rights to the fight card whose supporting bout between welterweights Roberto Duran and Carlos Palomino may have produced more ticket buyers than the main event. Holmes was so overwhelmingly favored that bookmakers refused to take bets on the match.

The Duran-Palomino bout was as good as expected, but the Holmes-Weaver contest turned out to be more than worth the price of admission by itself. Fighting well beyond his advertised mediocrity, Weaver rocked Holmes several times with vicious right hands and made things hard for the champion right up to the time Larry pulled it out with an eleventh round stoppage.

I was at ringside as a guest of promoter Don King. We had maintained a decent working relationship in spite of all the past disagreements. Watching Weaver give Holmes so much trouble made me confident that I had what it took to separate Larry from his WBC belt.

If Weaver could hurt him with a muscle-bound right hand, I knew I could knock him out with one of my trademark bombs.

When reporters asked for a post-fight comment, I made it short and to the point: "I'll destroy him."

As I exited the Garden, I was introduced to Frank Stallone, the brother of actor Sylvester Stallone. Frank informed me that the role of the main opponent in his brother's latest saga of

Rocky Balboa, *Rocky III*, had not yet been cast, and he thought that I would fit the part and should consider auditioning for it. I told him the real heavyweight title, not the "reel" one, was all I had in mind trying out for then, but if the opportunity to swap choreographed punches with his brother was still open later, I'd be happy to consider it.

Actually I had other issues on my mind. I was in the process of acquiring my dream house. The victory over Norton gave me enough money for a down payment on a mansion in Mecca, Ohio, just a few miles from Warren. This place was fit for a king. Hell, it was a kingdom in itself. Growing up, I had dreamed of living someday in a large Southern Colonial mansion with white pillars out front. My mecca in Mecca was even better than that. It was like Never-Never Land. It took me almost a week to reach every room on the property.

Our new home was a French Normandy manor spread over 10 acres. I had my own private lake, stocked with catfish, bluegill, and bass. Deer roamed in our front yard.

The mansion had eight bedrooms, each with its own full bathroom complete with gold fixtures. My five daughters had their own rooms. There was also a sauna and a steam room. The entire property cost me about $575,000. Norton had provided the down payment, I told the press; Holmes would pay it off.

But you wouldn't have known that our family had finally arrived on Easy Street to watch La Verne keep her nose to the grindstone. She was from the old school. She still washed the dishes by hand and hung the laundry out on the clothesline. La Verne was never awed by material success, but the change in our circumstances gave her the chance to be a stay-at-home mother, which beat gold faucets hands down.

The six years that she worked at Packard Electric to help support the family were now a thing of the past. I knew the physical work never bothered her, but the hassles of dealing with babysitters and being away from our girls had been awful for La Verne. Our second-oldest daughter, Cindy, would constantly complain of illness and missed school on a regular basis. Eventually, Cindy admitted that she was faking it in order to spend more time with her mother. La Verne had always been a strong woman and wonderful mother to our daughters.

I was happy to reward her by providing my family with a nice lifestyle.

La Verne was the real boss in the family, and I owed a lot of my success to her strength. I would have given up boxing years earlier had it not been for La Verne. She made me stick with it through the years of small paydays and canceled fights. I'd argue with Frank Luca, but when La Verne spoke, my answer was always, "Yes, dear."

I was able to enjoy my dream home for only a few months before I had to leave for the Catskills in upstate New York to train for the fight against Holmes. I needed to win not only to be recognized as champion of the world, but now also to pay my monthly housekeeping bills. Just to heat my large indoor pool in the winter cost $400. It took all day to clean the sewers and two days to cut the lawn. My goal was to whip Holmes and then hold the title for a long time so I wouldn't have to worry about a $1,000 utility bill.

Money wasn't my only concern. Right after I ensconced my wife in Paradise, the rug was pulled out from under her by a friend who told La Verne about my ongoing affair with Veronica. La Verne was always a step ahead of me, and there wasn't a thing she didn't know about me. It was the first time I ever heard La Verne use profanity, and she used it quite well.

"You asshole!" she said. "How can you be out there messing around with another woman after all we've been through, you shithead! If you don't stop seeing that woman, I'm going to kill you." Somehow, "Yes, dear" didn't quite cut it that time.

As always, La Verne was no fool. The household bills were too big for her to just kick me to the curbside, and so instead she said the most painful thing I'd ever heard in my life.

"If you try to leave me, I'm going to leave with you," La Verne said, delivering a subtle message that no matter what, we were attached at the hip.

That's where it stood as I headed for training camp to prepare for Holmes. I knew that I had delivered a no-so-subtle message to him when I knocked out Norton in one round. Holmes saw me destroy the man who gave him a helluva fight for 15 rounds not too long before. I knew that since Holmes had won the WBC title, his confidence and ring skills could only have improved. But he knew that if I landed one mighty right hand on his chin, nothing else would matter, and all those years of struggling to make it to the big time would have been canceled out.

Sure, Holmes had pitched a shut-out in our first match, but since then the momentum had shifted in my direction. Who had looked more impressive in his last outing? I had chewed up and spit Ken Norton out in just over one minute. Holmes had beaten Mike Weaver, but "Hercules" had put him through the tortures of the damned first.

I think the Weaver battle took a little bit out of Larry. Afterward, Holmes told the press that he might have to postpone our fight due to a number of ailments. He complained of a perforated ear drum and hoarseness and maintained that he had been thumbed in the eye. He sure didn't sound like a guy looking forward to his next fight.

The problem for Larry was that if he failed to sign on the dotted line to defend against me, he risked forfeiting his title. After he passed a medical exam in Cleveland, the WBC gave Holmes two options: fight me or be stripped of the belt. He signed.

We set up training camp for nine weeks at the beautiful Concord Hotel located on Kiamesha Lake. My goal was to put myself in the same condition I was in for the Norton bout. Each morning began with a run of five miles, followed by agility exercises. After breakfast—four eggs, steak, all-beef bacon, whole wheat toast, and fruit—I walked another two miles to let the food properly digest. Then I returned to bed, or would either call or write a letter to my family.

In the afternoon I would work out and spar in the gym, and then swim or chop some wood. After dinner I would study fight films and be in bed by 9:30 p.m.

My sparring partners were a disparate but talented group of boxers. I had "HOLMES" emblazoned on their headgear, and the psychological spin it provided me made their jobs a little harder.

"When Earnie starts to bear down on you, sometimes it's just best to close your eyes and hope the good Lord is watching over you," Terry Nicopolis, one of my sparring partners, told *The Ring* magazine. Another one, Calvin Langston, said, "Before I came here, nobody ever put me down in the ring. Now, all I think about is how to stay up."

I also used the services of Phil Brown. Frank had to go all the way down to Louisiana to get him to spar with me. Brown was one of the world's top amateur heavyweights and had just lost a close decision to legendary Cuban Olympic gold medalist Teofilo Stephenson in the Pan-American games. Brown was cobra-like quick with a style similar to the champ's, and was vital to my preparation.

I had a good working relationship with all of my sparring partners, but I intentionally never got overly chummy with any of them. They were there for one reason—to get me in the best shape possible. I liked them all personally, but in the ring they took their lumps. That's what they got paid for.

It was a good, productive camp, and when we headed for Las Vegas 10 days before the fight, I was in prime shape physically and mentally, and as prepared as I could be for my second chance at boxing immortality.

CHAPTER FOURTEEN

Last Chance

Don King, boxing's Vesuvius of verbiage, billed my fight against Holmes on September 28, 1979, at Caesar's Palace in Las Vegas, as an "Epic Explosion" and "The Greatest Boxing Show on Earth." If that sounds a little understated for him, King told anyone who would listen that it was the biggest card he had ever produced. When some sportswriters looked puzzled at this and reminded him about the Foreman-Ali "Rumble in the Jungle," King stipulated that the Zaire event had indeed been his biggest fight and pointed out that this production consisted of four main-event caliber bouts which made it his biggest card to date.

ABC-TV had agreed to air three hours of prime-time boxing. That meant in addition to my fight, King had to put on a starry, attractive undercard featuring some of the ring's biggest names. He filled that bill, signing Sugar Ray Leonard, Roberto Duran, and knockout sensation Wilfredo Gomez. Trouble is, when you're dealing with the biggest names, you're also dealing with the biggest—and tenderest—egos.

With Ali, the people's champion, out of the picture, albeit just temporarily, boxing was in search of a new savior. There were plenty of self-appointed candidates, including the above-named guys and the WBC heavyweight titlist. If you didn't know any better, you might have been tempted to feel sorry for King as he ran around trying to smooth the ruffled psyches of these potential heirs to the Ali mantle. Holmes wasn't happy sharing the spotlight with Leonard and Duran. Leonard was upset that Duran was being advertised as pound-for-pound the best boxer in the sport. Duran was annoyed because

Leonard was getting a larger payday, and Gomez feared his bout wouldn't be shown live back in his homeland of Puerto Rico. Everybody had a beef, but in the end, as it always does, it all worked out perfectly for Don King.

A three-column photo of King appeared in the *Las Vegas Sun*. Above it was the headline, "Don King—World's Greatest Promoter." King couldn't have said it better himself.

"That tells it all," King said with a Cheshire cat grin. If it wasn't true, they couldn't print it, right? Whether he had elevated boxing to new heights was debatable, but King had raised the bar when it came to shameless self-promotion.

The Sports Pavilion at Caesar's Palace was packed, and I entered the ring first to thunderous applause. A sizable contingent from Warren was on hand, but the faces I recognized around ringside belonged to celebrities Diana Ross, Joe DiMaggio, and Cary Grant.

I had plenty of time to be star-struck, because Holmes kept me waiting for several minutes. It was the same ploy Foreman tried on Ali in Zaire, and it didn't work any better in Nevada. Finally, Larry's trademark song, "Ain't No Stoppin' Us Now," blared, and the champion made his grand entrance. Holmes greeted me at ring center and the stare-down began. Did he think I would wet my shorts? I had already been 12 rounds with Holmes, and I knew the man quite well. I even liked him.

You didn't have to be psychic to predict how the hostilities would start. Larry came out moving and snapping rapid left jabs. Sometimes he stepped in with his straight left for added power. I kept pressing forward trying to land punches. Holmes never moved straight at me or stepped directly back from me, but instead he used side-to-side movement to keep me off balance and in no position to land my heavy artillery. I had a difficult time getting my feet set to throw my right hand. Larry moved so well behind his left jab.

In the third round, one of those jabs landed with the thumb of his glove in my eye, and my vision went blurry. I saw three Larrys, and ended up swinging at the wrong one.

For the next three rounds I continued to stalk Larry. I missed with several looping bombs as Holmes kept moving to his right to avoid my lethal punches.

In the fifth round my left eye began to close. I didn't know it at the time, of course, but my retina had become detached. My vision remained blurred throughout the contest.

Things got bleaker in the next round when I received a cut over my right eye that would require stitches. The title was slipping further out of my grasp by the second.

The pattern continued for two minutes and 30 seconds of the seventh round. Holmes worsened the cut over my right eye with a left hook. But then the punch I had been trying to land all night finally found its mark. An overhand right caught Holmes flush on the button and down he went as if he'd suddenly been deboned. As I headed for a neutral corner, Holmes didn't stir.

I was the heavyweight champion of the world. All my troubles were finally over. It was the greatest feeling I'd ever had.

And it lasted for five whole seconds.

As I stood in the neutral corner, I saw Holmes' eyebrows start to twitch as he lay on the floor, and I knew it wasn't over yet.

Later he would describe the impact of that punch as being like having a flash from a camera go off in his face. It was picture-perfect, all right, but Larry was a cagey fighter. Even with a head full of pinwheels, when Holmes got up he began bouncing up and down on his toes, subtly putting distance between us as the ref tolled off the mandatory eight count. That move gained Holmes another valuable second or two before the fight resumed.

In the final 30 seconds of the round, I threw desperate haymakers in an attempt to end it for good. One more power shot would have closed the show. Holmes' eyes were still glazed, but he clinched and held on for dear life until the bell came to his rescue.

Larry owed his survival to his trainer, Richie Giachetti, one of the shrewdest cornermen in the business. I had met Giachetti years earlier through Don King. Richie was from Cleveland and had briefly helped train me when I was under contract to King. Back then, Richie drummed it into me that if I was ever knocked down I should shake my head to clear the dizziness and then move around to get my legs steady. That's contrary to what old-school trainers instruct their fighters, namely to take full advantage of the entire eight count on the canvas and then get up. Giachetti argued that when a fighter first gets up at eight, with only two seconds remaining in the count, he runs the risk of stumbling or looking dizzy enough for the referee to stop the fight. I never forgot those instructions and, unfortunately, neither did Larry.

The minute's rest further snapped Holmes out of it, and in round eight he was again moving and jabbing. I chased him, throwing more arcing bombs, but most were wildly off target. The next two rounds followed the same pattern, and fatigue was setting in.

A chant of "Earnie! Earnie!" filled the Pavilion. The crowd was behind me and tried to inspire me to finish strong. But Frank Luca had to help me off my stool to answer the bell for the tenth. My legs were unsteady, and I held my gloves low because of weariness. Quitting wasn't an option for me. A fighter's job is to fight and to take it.

The punishment continued in the eleventh round. A few times Larry punched me and then asked ref Davey Pearl to stop the contest. Blood from my cuts had crimsoned both of our trunks. I was exhausted, but I kept punching as best as I could. At times I even fell back into the ropes from exhaustion more than from anything Larry did.

The referee called for a brief time out in the middle of the eleventh round to examine me. I told him I wanted to continue. Pearl let the fight go on, but after Holmes landed two more punches Pearl called it off. I didn't protest.

The first one to comfort me was the champion. Larry came over and put his arms around my shoulder.

"I love you. You're a great fighter," he said.

"You're a man," I responded. "I love you, too, Larry. Thanks."

I've always counted Larry Holmes as a good friend. That's hard to find in the fight game because of all the backstabbing that goes on. Everyone is so jealous of one another, but Larry and I always stayed above that. We were competitive come fight time, but outside the ropes he knew he could count on me being in his corner. And I could count on him being a gentleman after he knocked the crap out of me.

Years after I fought him for the title, Holmes invited me to help him raise money for one of the youth programs he supported in Pennsylvania. It was a race called "Run with the Champion," and I beat Larry. "I had to beat you at something," I joked.

After our fight, I emerged from my dressing room with my arm around La Verne. After appearing at a post-fight press conference we jumped into the back of a police car for a quick trip to the hospital. The cut over my right eye required 29 stitches. But it was my swollen-shut left eye that would soon cause me more serious problems.

In the meantime, I got a kick out of a story making the rounds that when Don King saw his undefeated meal ticket Holmes on the deck in the seventh round, he jumped up from his front-row seat and stuck his cigar back in his mouth lighted end first. He was definitely blowing a lot of smoke that night!

I announced my retirement from boxing after the Holmes fight. My heart was no longer in the sport, or so I thought. In fact, it was getting spread pretty thin outside the ring, too. My affair with Veronica was still going full-force, and she wasn't the only one. As a top heavyweight contender, I had more gorgeous women at my disposal than I had ever imagined could be possible. I chased a few of them, and they weren't as hard to catch as Larry Holmes was.

It was wrong, but becoming a celebrity can change a person. I had always lived a clean life, never smoking or drinking and drugging. But pretty women were another matter. Most of the ones I messed with, I can't even remember their names. But that wasn't important to them, either.

"Honey," they'd say, "are you looking for romancing? Because I'm looking for financing."

I was a sucker for that kind of transaction. I'm not proud of it and especially regret that I hurt so many good people along the way. La Verne was at the top of that list, of course. She knew about my affairs, which resulted in three children not born to La Verne and me—Catherine, Natasha, and Earnie, Jr. I love them just as much as I do any of my other children, and sadly, they never got the chance to live with me as they were growing up. That's the price you pay for a wandering eye.

La Verne still wanted us to work things out, and I agreed to give it another chance.

It was the same with boxing, but not because I had emotional ties to the sport—I needed money. The Holmes payday had been good, but not enough to retire on. Especially with my mortgage payments. I had also invested a sizable sum in gold, but it turned out to be "fool's gold." I had seen an advertisement in a magazine for gold Krugerrands. I went to see the dealer myself and paid $55,000 in cash. When I sold it, I tripled my money. I tried another dealer in Youngstown from a coin shop, but with very different results. It was no good. But when it came time to collect, the owner had vanished with my funny money, and I was out of some serious cash.

Before I could get back in the ring, I had to deal with the scariest problem of all. After the swelling in my left eye had healed, I was still having vision problems. I was seeing black spots, and when I saw an eye specialist in Warren, he sent me right to Cleveland to another specialist. That meant trouble.

The doctor in Cleveland bounced me to Dr. Ronald Michels, a world-renowned eye specialist at Johns Hopkins University in Baltimore, Maryland. Michels was due to fly to Russia, but delayed his trip to examine my eye. The very next day I was in surgery for five hours to repair my detached retina.

I stayed at Johns Hopkins for a week and did nothing but rest the whole time. Dr. Michels informed me that my left eye would end up stronger than the right, and assured me that I would be able to fight again without risking another injury to the eye. While I spent about six weeks lying around, doing basically nothing, rumors began to spread within the boxing world that I was blind in left eye. But I announced that I was coming back with two good eyes, and eventually I signed up to box Colombian contender Bernardo Mercado on March 8, 1980, at the Playboy Club in Great Gorge, New Jersey.

Ideally, I would've started back against a series of ham-and-eggers, but the taxman was on my tail and I needed a fast score. The Internal Revenue Service presented me with a $1 million bill for back taxes on my fights.

Mercado had an impressive record of 25-2 with 22 knockouts. His losses were to Big John Tate and Mike Weaver, two formidable foes. Mercado had come to the fore two years earlier when Muhammad Ali traveled to Bogota for an exhibition with him, and Mercado had given him five competitive rounds.

I worked myself into decent enough shape for this contest, but came in five pounds over my ideal fighting weight. The first few rounds were even, then in the third I began to pull ahead and floored Mercado for an eight count. Near the end of the round, I caught Mercado with an uppercut. It was a solid punch, but one of Mercado's teeth caused a tear in my glove. It wasn't detected until the fourth round. Once the referee noticed, he interrupted the fight to order that the damaged glove be replaced. It took several minutes for a new glove to be rounded up and put on—long enough for the momentum I'd been building to fizzle.

When the action finally resumed, I was all cooled off and could not pick up where I'd left off. Mercado, on the other hand, benefited from the unscheduled break and started coming on. The referee eventually stopped the contest in the seventh round, giving Mercado a technical knockout victory.

It had been a hell of a year, but as tempting as the idea was, I could hardly dig myself a hole and crawl in, because I was already in the hole too deep financially. What I needed was money, and lots of it—as fast as I could make it. And the only legal way I knew to do it involved lacing on the gloves and going back to work.

CHAPTER FIFTEEN

Early Retirement

Financial help suddenly appeared in the form of boxing pro-moter Harold Smith. Smith was taking the boxing world by storm, attempting to supplant Don King and Bob Arum as the sport's top promoter. Smith lavished exorbitant paydays on mediocre heavyweights like Marty Monroe and Scott LeDoux, and even bigger ones on aging contenders like Ken Norton and myself. Smith also attempted to get Larry Holmes under contract in hopes of gaining total control of the heavyweight title. He was a man with a plan.

Smith's organization, called Muhammad Ali Professional Sports (MAPS), had promoted seven bouts in 1979 that lost thousands of dollars each. But when he offered me hefty purses for matches with Le Roy Boone and Randall "Tex" Cobb, I was too strapped to refuse. I was glad I didn't when I met with Smith and an associate of his in a Las Vegas hotel room, and Harold paid me $100,000 in cash as a signing bonus. I sat right there and counted it in front of both men. Every single bill. I wanted to make sure that they weren't using the old trick of putting a few C-notes on top of a stack of $1 bills. It took me a few hours to count it all, but when I finished, I happily signed a contract with Smith.

My first bout under the MAPS banner took place on June 14, 1980, in Cincinnati. I wasn't in peak boxing condition for Boone because he had been stopped by Marty Monroe and Gerry Cooney, the only recognizable names on his ledger, and there-fore didn't seem to be much to worry about. Was I ever wrong.

The sparse crowd on hand got its money's worth that night. Boone and I had a 10-round barn-burner. Luckily, I paced myself and was awarded a unanimous decision victory. Although it was an entertaining card, less than $3,000 came in at the gate. It was another financial kick in the ass for Smith, but he didn't seem bothered at all and kept right on paying out top dollar, which was all that mattered to me. As long as those checks cleared, he was my dear, dear friend.

At age 36, I was ranked fifth by the WBC, and my lengthy professional log now tallied 59-9-1, with 56 KOs. I figured Tex Cobb for an easy number 57, for no other reason than I'd never heard of the guy before. I wish I could still say that.

Cobb, I discovered soon enough, was a massive physical specimen, 6-foot-3 and 230 pounds going into our contest. He had played football for two years at Abilene Christian and claimed to have majored in probation. He was undefeated at 16-0, with all of his victories tallied against an assortment of unknowns. Tex only had a limited amateur background and was being moved carefully by his management. I didn't know if he could fight, but I found out he was one of the funniest people around.

"I only had two fights as an amateur and lost both of them," he once said. "I figure I didn't have much of a future there—so I turned pro."

I had originally been scheduled to fight another protected white contender, Gerry Cooney, but he had pulled out due to a back injury. In retrospect, I wish it was Cooney I had faced. There is no way he could've been tougher than Tex Cobb.

We fought in Detroit on August 2, 1980, as a supporting bout beneath the WBA welterweight title fight of champion Pipino Cuevas against local hero Thomas "Hit Man" Hearns.

The unbeaten Hearns had revived boxing in Detroit, the city that had produced world champions Joe Louis and Sugar Ray Robinson. Hearns and his stablemates on the Kronk Boxing Team had turned the Motor City into one of the best live-gate sites for boxing in the country.

While the Hit Man had understandably received most of the pre-fight press, I got a warm welcome from the big crowd when I entered the ring. I had on brand-new shoes, and as I moved around waiting for the bell, I noticed the mat felt slippery.

The next thing I noticed was that Tex Cobb had a head like granite, and he could do some hitting of his own. Tex and

I slugged it out at ring center throughout the opening round. I banked several hard right hands off his chin and figured it was only a matter of time before I dropped this giant. Later, Cobb told reporters that hearing the bell end the first round sent him into an emotional tailspin because he realized there were nine more rounds to go.

The truth is that I wasn't too happy about that myself. Cobb absorbed every hard shot I threw. And in my new shoes I was slipping a lot and having trouble planting my feet to get maximum power behind my punches. That's not an excuse, though, because Cobb would have caused me trouble had we been fighting barefoot in a field of clover. He was a sponge when it came to taking punches, but then came right back to dish out his own vicious shots. And an occasional quip on top of it.

I remember early on when I had him tied up in a clinch. The referee separated us and scolded me for holding on to Tex. Whereupon Cobb, a big grin on his face, said to the ref, "Leave the man alone, can't you see he's busy?"

What wasn't so funny was when Cobb busted my jaw with a wicked left hook in the eighth round. I knew it was broken right away because of the excruciating pain. The referee stopped the fight, awarding Cobb a technical knockout victory. My jaw was wired shut for the next six weeks.

Although it was a bad day for me, it was a monumental one for Harold Smith. MAPS added two new champions to its roster when Aaron Pryor defeated Antonio Cervantes to capture the WBA junior welterweight crown in Cincinnati, and after my fight with Cobb, Hearns knocked out Cuevas to capture the 147-pound crown.

Harold Smith seemed too good to be true, which is how it turned out. Less than a year after the Cobb fight, Smith—a.k.a. Ross Fields—was charged with the embezzlement of over $21 million from the Wells Fargo Bank of California.

It was the largest embezzlement in U.S. history, and Smith would serve more than five years in federal prison for it. I avoided being dragged in on the case by the merest technicality. In May 1981, the FBI came knocking on my door to ask about the $100,000 I took from Smith a few months earlier. Specifically, they wanted to know if I had ever met with

Smith in a hotel room in Cleveland and collected $100,000 from him there.

"That's a lie," I told them. That seemed to satisfy them and they told me to have a nice day. The meeting lasted all of 30 seconds. Of course, had they asked me if I'd met with Smith in Las Vegas and collected $100,000 in cash, I would have told them that was what happened. But I didn't think it was my business to provide the FBI with a lesson in geography.

Well, now I knew where Smith got all that scratch he liked to throw around. I'm not endorsing grand theft, mind you, but I'm not going to tell you that I wasn't sorry to see Smith, or whatever his name was, get carted off to jail. He treated us fairly and paid us outrageously, even if it wasn't his money. It might have been a black eye for boxing, but it was a fat paycheck for those of us taking the punches.

The paydays from my two MAPS fights had been good, but with MAPS down for the count I was in serious financial straits again. Then I received a phone call that gave me a glimmer of hope. It was an agent calling on behalf of movie star Sylvester Stallone.

Stallone was still searching for someone to play Clubber Lang, the principal antagonist for *Rocky III*, and, like his brother Frank, he thought I'd be right for the part. I flew out to Hollywood a few days later to meet Stallone and give acting a shot.

When I arrived, I was chauffeured to the boxing gym to meet Stallone. What surprised me right off the bat was his size, or rather the lack of it. He looks much bigger on the silver screen. After some chit-chat I got dressed in my boxing gear and climbed into the ring to spar with Stallone. This was to be my audition for the movie, me against Rocky Balboa. Trouble was, he looked like a middleweight.

We started to move around in the ring, feeling each other out. Stallone threw a couple of punches, then I hit him with a jab followed by a right hand. There wasn't much steam behind them. I knew this was only a tryout, and the last thing I wanted to do was hurt Sly because I really wanted the part. But Stallone halted the action, put his head down for a second, and then looked at me.

"Earnie, I want this to look real," he said. "Open up with your punches." Guess he was talking about cinéma vérité, but on the chance that the heavyweight box-office champion of Hollywood didn't realize what he was asking for, I continued to pull my punches. So Stallone again stopped things, and this time he looked annoyed.

"Look Earnie, I don't use any stunt men in my place," he said. "I want this to look real. They say you are a good puncher, so show me."

This time I did as directed. The first opening I saw, I caught Stallone with a solid right to the body. Cut! He doubled over, holding his sides. Suddenly, the "Italian Stallion" looked more like a horse that needed to be put out to pasture. When he could finally talk again, Sly said, "Earnie, after much thought, I don't think the public will buy me beating you in the ring." My audition was over.

Soon after came one of the most difficult periods of my life. I took the money out of the bank on my fool's gold investment once I realized it was a scam. I had gotten burned for about $7,500, but the press blew it out of proportion, reporting that I had passed a worthless check for $10,000. According to some accounts, I'd gone to jail. In fact, I was home the entire time.

But pretty soon I no longer had a home. The Internal Revenue Service slapped me with a 1979 tax claim for $172,043, and my debt to Trumbull Savings and Loan came to more than $71,000. I could have declared bankruptcy, but I didn't feel that was right. So in April 1981, I let the bank foreclose on the Mecca estate and it was sold at a sheriff's sale to cover my mounting debt.

The $1 million-plus I had earned in the ring was all gone. I had learned the hard way that you can't keep up with the Joneses when the Joneses own the bank.

My troubles grew when the IRS turned up the heat regarding the $1 million I owed them in back taxes. In desperation I turned to Don King, who always employed the best lawyers to defend him against the myriad of legal actions brought against him. He didn't let me down. King recommended Joe Krush, a former IRS agent with nine years of service. Once I hired Krush, he resolved my matters quickly with the IRS.

That put a million-dollar smile on my face.

I got a second chance at Hollywood when out of the blue I was called by actor Jackie Gleason. He was a huge fight fan, and he wondered if I'd be interested in making a cameo appearance in *Smokey and the Bandit II*, the film Gleason and Burt Reynolds were doing together. After making sure that there would be no fight scenes between me and Gleason, I said sure thing.

My scene was shot in an underground tunnel in Atlanta, where Gleason and his incompetent but good-hearted son try to steal my car to keep chasing the Bandit, played by Reynolds. I catch them in the act and react to their lame excuses by flattening both of them.

It was great. It was funny. It got left on the cutting room floor.

However, I did get paid $5,000 a day plus expenses for the shoot, which made me a happy camper.

"Jackie, if you need me, you got the number," I told Gleason. "Call me anytime you don't want me to be in your movie again." How sweet it was!

Since it was becoming apparent that I was not about to make anyone forget about Billy Dee Williams, I turned again to the only sure-fire way I knew how to make a buck.

On October 17, 1980, I knocked out somebody in a fight in West Palm Beach, Florida. The only thing I'm sure about is that it happened in the second round. Most official records list the guy as Ted Hamilton, but it might have been Ted Wadkins. Whoever he was, he agreed to fight at the last minute when somebody else took a powder rather than face me, which wasn't that unusual. When that happens and there are customers in the seats and money in the till, a promoter almost has no choice but to find whatever live body is available to fill in.

It really didn't matter much to me. At this point, I didn't have any goals in boxing except providing added income for my family. Hell, yes, I'd have preferred to go up against the top dogs, but I wasn't exactly in a position to call the shots. As long as I still had major name recognition in boxing, I was going to take full advantage of it.

I was recruited to fight on some shows promoted by one of the Toughman founders, Art Dore. Dore was based out of

Bay City, Michigan, and was arranging bouts for his boxer, United States Boxing Association light heavyweight champion Murray Sutherland. I worked out an agreement with Dore to make a celebrity appearance at several Toughman contests and to fight on two Michigan cards headlined by Sutherland. The first was on July 29, 1981, against Terrill Sims.

First, I had to pass a battery of tests to determine that my surgically repaired left eye was fit for battle. When the doctor came in I suggested a shortcut that would save us both a lot of time. I told him my own doctor tested the eye by pinning a $100 bill and a $1 bill on the wall and then having me stand 30 feet away with my right eye covered and pick out the $ 100 bill, which I got to pocket if did so correctly.

Unfortunately, the Michigan doctor used the standard eye chart. I still passed with flying colors.

Two-and-a-half years before I had knocked out Harold Carter in three rounds in the Saginaw Civic Center. This time it took only me two to flatten Sims. But I was rusty and overanxious. I had only trained three days for the fight and weighed in at a career-high 225 pounds. Instead of training, I was spending most of my time on the janitorial service I'd started as a means of regular income.

A few weeks later I knocked out Mike Rodger on another Art Dore promotion. Dore's events were always entertaining. He had a few of his Toughman champions boxing in the prelims. They may not have been artful practitioners of the sweet science, but they gave the crowd plenty to cheer about with their face-first approach to boxing.

I was in Vegas to watch Larry Holmes defend his world title against Trevor Berbick. As I was leaving town afterward, I had a chance encounter at the airport that would change my life. As I exited a limousine, I was approached by a gentleman.

"Hey, I know you," he said. "You're Isaac Hayes."

"Sorry," I told him. "Wrong brother."

The man then introduced himself as Jimmy Adams, who was involved somehow with professional wrestling. We struck up a pleasant conversation, and the next thing I knew we were exchanging phone numbers. Adams phoned me a few days later and he even came to visit me in Ohio. We really hit it off.

Although Adams admittedly knew nothing about boxing, he thought we could work together well. However, he lived in Martinsville, Virginia, and had no desire to relocate. After some thought, I was open to the idea of moving. I wanted a fresh start, and I was convinced my janitorial service could do well in Virginia. In fact, Adams said that with his help it was a sure thing. What he forgot to mention was that he knew even less about that kind of business than he did about boxing.

Known as "A City Without Limits," Martinsville is a town of about 20,000 residents located in the foothills of the Blue Ridge Mountains. When I visited I found the atmosphere was warm and friendly, and Adams convinced me that he had connections in business and boxing. He had once been a bodyguard for actor Robert Duvall, and was supposedly road manager for country singer Hank Williams Jr.

With the mansion in Mecca gone, we decided to start all over again in Martinsville, and took up residence in the Lakewood Forest area.

The move was hard on the girls, but I didn't spend much time pining for the mansion and its huge financial burden. I was glad that part of my life was past. Now I was working to pay my debts and I was feeling good about life again. No matter what, I always tried to maintain a good attitude. There are lots of curves in the road of life, and after what we'd been through, we deserved a nice, long stretch of straightaway.

That went mostly for La Verne, whose problems didn't all come with dollar signs on them. I was still involved with Veronica even though we would only see each other about three times a year. She gave birth to a daughter named Lisa on February 20, 1980. You don't have to guess who the daddy was.

Neither did La Verne. In fact, she found out about the baby before I did. I won't repeat the names she called me in case there are minors reading this. But La Verne stuck with me.

So did Veronica when I told her about the move to Virginia.

"You gotta do what's right for you and your family," she said. "And I will wait for you for 10 years if you want me to." Like I said before, she was a no-pressure woman.

In Martinsville, Adams introduced me to several terrific people. One was his lawyer, Ben Gardner, who also happened to be a boxing fan. Gardner and I hit it off right away. He was a longtime resident of Martinsville, known and widely respected by the entire community.

Ben aided me with advice on investments, tax shelters, and negotiating fight contracts. In exchange for his legal services, I made him a member of my boxing entourage, which thrilled him to no end. Ben was happy just being in charge of my spit bucket, and worked in my corner for my next several fights. When Don King came calling a few months later, I had Ben negotiate my next purse with him.

I also opened a cleaning supply business called Knock Out Janitorial Supply, Inc., in partnership with Adams. At the same time I purchased a trailer park, but that turned out to be a short-time investment, because I hated having to collect rent from people who did not want to pay it.

After I got settled I also struck up a friendship, through Adams, with wrestler Big John Studd. Studd was a boxing fan, too, and it just so happened that I was his personal favorite. As our friendship grew, Studd sounded me out about joining him on the pro wrasslin' circuit. I wouldn't have been the first boxer to go that route. Former heavyweight champs Primo Carnera and Joe Louis had done it to make some desperately needed money. But I frankly wasn't that desperate. I had nothing against wrestling, and proved it by becoming a referee. It was $500 for just 15 minutes of work, and I also had the best seat in the house.

I enjoyed the camaraderie the wrestlers shared in the locker room. They were a fun group of guys. However, some of their fans were a totally different story. I remember one time while in Atlanta, this fragile-looking little old gray-haired lady sporting a bun and granny glasses had a special surprise for Studd. This old dame who looked like she should have been home baking pecan pies to raise money for her church pulled a gun on him because she believed he was fighting dirty against her guy. She actually threatened to shoot Studd right between the eyes.

As third man in the ring, my job, obviously, was to maintain order. When things got out of control, I would naturally resort to fisticuffs, laying out the big, tough bad guys with the sort of phony punching that Sylvester Stallone had wanted no part of. Some of the wrestlers expressed reluctance to have me work their matches because they didn't want to get nailed by an accidentally genuine blow.

Backstage before each match, I would work with the wrestler I was going to "KO" later, rehearsing the big blow. The trick in these situations is to pull back your fist the second you feel the chin of the other guy. It sounds easy enough, but when you've been whacking people on the chin as long as I had and meaning it, going the other way took some getting used to.

Fact is, once in a while I slipped and really followed through on a punch or two, which is what cut short my career as a wrestling referee.

Jimmy Adams was a country and western fan, and we would take trips to Nashville often. On our first trip there, we went to see singer Conway Twitty. After the show, Jimmy and I were invited backstage where we also met Jean Shepard, known as the "Grand Lady of the Grand Ole Opry." Shepard had been a member of the Opry for 25 years and is considered a living legend in Nashville. She had charted numerous country hits and her husband, Benny Birchfield, was also a prominent member of the local music community.

They were also very nice people, and Shepard and Birchfield insisted that Jimmy and I stay the night at their mansion even though we had just met. I thanked them for the offer, explaining that Jimmy and I had already checked into a hotel, but they wouldn't take no for an answer. So we checked out of the hotel and into the mansion.

The next morning I woke up early and went for a run. Neighbors politely waved as I jogged past their beautifully appointed homes. I don't think they had a clue as to who I was, but I reasoned they were just being hospitable. When I returned to the mansion, I complimented Jean and Benny on the friendliness of the neighborhood.

"They must have thought you were leaving, Earnie," Benny said, bursting out with laughter.

Jimmy also introduced me to legendary singer George "No Show" Jones, and I ended up doing executive protection for him. One of my main jobs was to make sure that "No Show," who got the nickname for missing many scheduled performances in his heavy drinking and drugging days, showed.

It was while I was on assignment with Jones at the Grand Ole Opry Hotel that I received the offer to fight on the undercard of Muhammad Ali's comeback bout against Trevor Berbick on December 11, 1981, in Nassau. I was promised $50,000 to fight the no-hope opponent who turned out to be Jeff Sims. It was an offer I couldn't refuse.

It had been awhile since my last bout, and I made plans to set up training camp about 65 miles south of Martinsville in Winston-Salem, North Carolina, under new trainer Whit Lowery. I met Lowery through Adams and had watched him work with his fighters. I was very impressed with how he taught boxing the old-fashioned way. Instead of ragging on me to knock guys out with one punch, Lowery encouraged me to work on my jab, footwork, and combinations. Maybe I wasn't too old to learn some new tricks.

I remember how out of shape I felt my first day back in the gym. Every heavyweight there wanted to spar with me. What they really wanted was to boost their reputations by beating up a fat, old ex-contender. I huffed and puffed through six rounds of sparring that first day. Although I was tired beyond belief, I was able to land a heavy punch when it was needed. Afterward I promised all the young lions an opportunity to get a piece of me if they would give me 10 days to get my wind back. Ten days later, it seemed that every other heavyweight in Winston-Salem had lost his way to the gym, and I had to hire some professional sparring partners in order to complete training.

While I was training in Winston-Salem, I let Adams run my janitorial business. I genuinely liked Jimmy, but found out the hard way we had no business being in business together.

Whit and I left for the Bahamas two weeks before the fight. We found a sad scene in Nassau, especially where Ali was concerned. He should have stayed retired. I knew others said the same about me, but Ali showed visible signs of decline both in and out of the ring. The most alarming was that he noticeably slurred his words. His overall movement was much slower, and clearly Ali was in no condition to even spar in the gym, much less have a real fight with a strong bull like Trevor Berbick.

A palpable air of negativity enveloped the promotion. All three major U.S. television networks turned down the opportunity to air the card, something that had never happened to Ali before. Even Muhammad's mother openly pleaded for her 40-year-old son to retire. But we all have to make up our own minds about what's best for us, and in my case what was best was collecting $50,000 to fight a stiff, even when my opponent changed from a stiff to some stiff competition in the person of young Jeff Sims.

Welcoming him to the big time with a fifth-round KO helped me decide that, given the thin talent in the heavyweight ranks at that time, I might just as well keep going and see what happened. But first I had to collect my 50 grand, which almost resulted in a second fight that night.

The promoter of Ali-Berbick was a man named James Cornelius. After the fight, Cornelius complained to everyone about how much money he had lost on the deal. I wasn't in the mood for a sob story, especially when he got to the part about not having enough cash to pay me. At that point I locked the door, waved a fist at Cornelius and his money man, and promised that unless he was Spiderman, no one was getting out of that room until I left first with what had been promised me. Moments later, Cornelius miraculously came up with my money.

"Earnie, you fought the best fight out there," he said. Then he turned to his accountant and said, "Pay him."

My comeback continued at the Grand Traverse Hilton in Traverse City, Michigan, a small but beautiful tourist town. At age 37, l was climbing into the ring with another determined prospect, unbeaten Michigan state champion Ali Haakim. He fought under the prestigious Kronk banner and had Emanuel Steward in his corner. The 15-0 Haakim talked plenty of trash at the weigh-in, referring to me as the "Old Man." It was pretty feeble stuff, and I made a point of letting Haakim know I fully aimed to be his daddy in the ring.

I suspected that the kid's brave talk actually was more for his own benefit than mine and was intended to cover up a pretty good case of fright. That was borne out when Haakim did his best to avoid me throughout our fight. I might as well have been his daddy, the way he hugged me for all 10 rounds. When I did manage to extricate myself from his death grip, with no help from the strangely silent referee, I landed enough punches to win a unanimous decision and break Haakim's jaw and ear drum.

The kid talked a good fight, but even his own trainer recognized that it was time for him to find a less dangerous way to make a living.

"Based on the way he [Haakim] boxed tonight, he should quit," Emanuel Steward told the *Traverse City Record-Eagle*. "There's no place in boxing for a guy without heart. It's not a sport where you can say, 'I'll sit on the bench and let someone else play.'"

I was ready to play again in just two weeks, after an old friend unexpectedly called to inquire about my availability. Don King was promoting a show in Dallas for HBO headlined by Salvador Sanchez defending his world featherweight title against Jorge Garcia. Although Dallas wasn't exactly a boxing hotbed, Don felt it might develop into something along those lines. King had some HBO dollars to lighten his financial risk, and he asked me to fight on the card to help sell tickets. I must say, I felt honored; but I had learned from my past errors. This time, I had King negotiate with the man who held my spit bucket, my attorney Ben Gardner. They reached an agreement, and it was set for me to fight another comebacking ex-contender, Joe Bugner, who'd once gone the distance against Ali in a title fight.

King also asked Larry Holmes to box an exhibition on the card to boost interest in Holmes' upcoming title defense against Gerry Cooney. Now 39-0, Larry had registered 11 successful title defenses and had ruled the heavyweight division longer than any champion since Joe Louis. But he still had not captured the public's imagination. Larry was a class person, an excellent role model, but that wasn't enough for the media, which had been spoiled by the charisma of Muhammad Ali. Other black athletes like O.J. Simpson, "Mean" Joe Greene, and Sugar Ray Leonard had penetrated the TV commercial market, but Larry was invisible. As a friend, I know how much it bothered Larry.

At the same time, the press was going nuts over Gerry Cooney as it had over no heavyweight since Ali himself, even though the Irish giant had been more protected than the Brinks payroll. His one-round knockout and near-decapitation of ancient former heavyweight champion Ken Norton was on sports highlight reels for weeks. Cooney had a powerful left hook, no doubt about it; but his biggest asset seemed to be the color of his skin.

Joe Bugner had also gone the distance with Joe Frazier in his previous boxing life, but since then his Limey chin hadn't aged too well and, in spite of my years, I was punching as hard as ever. In Dallas I knocked him down with a right uppercut in the first round and cut him wide open with an overhand right in the second. After inspecting the damage, the physician stopped the contest. Bugner protested, but it was the correct decision. He would have been horizontal within another round or two. I was, after all, "the hardest puncher in modern times." That's what Don King told the media, and if you couldn't believe the "World's Greatest Promoter," who could you believe?

CHAPTER SIXTEEN

Have Gloves, Will Travel

Sugar Ray Leonard was the top attraction in boxing at this time. His September 1981 knockout of Thomas Hearns at Caesar's Palace generated over $37 million in revenue, but the June 11, 1982, heavyweight bout between Larry Holmes and Gerry Cooney would shatter those numbers. I intended to do a little shattering myself when I met contender James "Quick" Tillis on the undercard.

Tillis had recently blown an opportunity to claim the WBA heavyweight title by coasting against Mike Weaver in a 15-round bout. Weaver could've been taken, and even Angelo Dundee in Tillis' own corner was upset by his man's refusal or inability to put it into top gear with the title on the line.

"Quick" entered our contest with a record of 21-1, and was a top-10 ranked heavyweight. Even though at 38 I had been written off by most boxing scribes, I was fighting in the richest promotion in the history of boxing. If I landed one of my bombs with the whole world watching, I'd be back in the money.

Tillis made sure to stay on his toes and away from my punching range. The parking lot where the ring was situated at Caesar's Palace was hot. I hoped the heat would wear down my non-stop opponent who was logging big mileage while staying on the run. Tillis threw speedy flurries, then retreated. I attempted to cut off the ring throughout our contest. I landed some power shots, but never flush. Near the bell at the end of the second I landed some good belts. I was penalized a point in the fourth round for an accidental shot that landed moments after the bell. Tillis was piling up the points while staying on the run. Then in the ninth round ... WHAM! I landed one of my patented right hands to Tillis' jaw. Down went Tillis. The crowd at Caesar's Palace exploded in unison.

"Quick" was laid face-first on the canvas. Momentarily, I was back in the title hunt. Then Tillis stirred and regained consciousness. He barely beat the count of 10, but beat it he did. Tillis later described that punch in his autobiography:

> I'll never forget the effect that hit took on me. I'd walked into the Land of Make-Believe. Some fighters hear harps playing, some see the Day of Judgment or just plain darkness. For me, it was saxophones and trombones sounding in my ear with one low-pitched note. Eeeeeeeeeeeeeee, all one note, like a bagpiper who fell over dead with no one to stop the last note. As the note rang in my ear, I saw little blue rats scamper out to smoke cigarettes and eat Spam sandwiches.

After I beat the count, he continued to move and box until the final bell. Quick received the decision, but I was the clearly the sentimental favorite as the crowd booed the verdict. I had been badly cut over my right eye in the fight. The skin of a 38-year-old pugilist isn't as elastic as that of the younger warriors.

In the main event, Holmes put on a career performance by stopping Cooney in the 13th round. Holmes and Cooney each pocketed over $8 million. A payday like that can get a guy over a few rough spots.

Later that night, I was walking around Caesar's Palace with La Verne and Ben Gardner when Ben noticed the actor called Mr. T from afar. Mr. T, whose real name is Lawrence Tureaud, was in full Mandinka warrior regalia, with his unique hairstyle, military boots, and gold jewelry hanging everywhere. He was well-known to the Caesar's fight crowd, and it was largely thanks to me, because "T," as everyone called him, had gotten the role of Clubber Lang in *Rocky III* that I'd blown by whacking Sly Stallone too hard.

As we got closer, La Verne called out to him by his real first name, Lawrence. Mr. T saw her and immediately dropped his trademark glower and swept her up in a big hug.

When Ben wondered what was going on, I explained that when I was in charge of Don King's fight camp a few years earlier, Mr. T had been a bodyguard there for Leon Spinks. Since the camp in Windsor, Ohio, wasn't far from Warren, La Verne and I had had Leon and Lawrence over to the house for a few cookouts. After that, of course, I made him a star. That, and the fact that he was magnificent as Clubber Lang.

My own star was definitely on the decline. But the name Earnie Shavers still had some marquee value, and I was booked to fight in Houston just 11 days after the loss to Tillis. My record was 67-11-1. My knockout-to-win percentage topped the charts at .940, and only George Foreman was in the same league with a .933 KO-to-win ratio.

There was a problem, though, with the Texas fight. I'd incurred a 10-stitch cut against Tillis, and the doctor said it would be three weeks before I could even spar again. I hated to miss a payday, but thanks to La Verne I didn't have to. When we returned from Las Vegas, she had me apply an aloe vera product to my wound three times a day. She told me that the cut would be healed within a week. I thought she was crazy, but I figured I had nothing to lose and gave it a shot. Sure enough, a week later the cut was healed.

The boxing commission in Texas knew about the injury I'd received in the Tillis fight, but an examination disclosed no reason to keep me out of the ring.

My Houston opponent, Billy Joe Thomas, had previously been defeated by Ed "Too Tall" Jones, the Dallas Cowboy football player turned heavyweight wannabe. So there was little to fear from him, and he went out in five rounds.

After the fight, I got a call from the owner of Sasco, an aloe vera company based in Dallas. I had been quoted in the papers about the miraculous healing properties of aloe vera, and, having gotten wind of my comments, the man wanted me to become head celebrity spokesman for his company. La Verne, Ben Gardner, and I were flown to Dallas and the poobah greeted us at the airport in person. He whisked us off to the aloe vera factory in a limo, and I began to envision myself, slathered in aloe vera, hawking the stuff on every TV in the country.

We got a deluxe tour of the facility, and the guy told me he would give me $25,000 as a signing bonus and a hefty weekly salary to be his pitchman. It was not a problem for me. Once the discussion moved to the board room, I let Gardner take over. He negotiated a lucrative contract for me to be the aloe vera poster boy. Farewell, nasty, stinking, sweaty world of boxing!

Then, no sooner had we arrived back in Martinsville, I received word that the aloe vera company decided to withdraw its offer, with no explanation.

Hello again, nasty, stinking, sweaty world of boxing! Seven weeks later I was in Lafayette, Louisiana, to box New Orleans-based journeyman Walter Santemore. He'd been Gerry Cooney's sparring partner for the Holmes fight, and rumor had it that Santemore had looked impressive working with "Gentleman Gerry." I didn't know much more than that about Walt, but I knew it would be a big win for him if he could beat me. Boxing in his home state, with Cooney on hand to cheer him on, Santemore had all the motivation he needed.

My own mind was far from the fight. I had just been indicted days earlier in federal district court on two counts of federal tax evasion. I really needed whatever money I could command by putting myself in front of young lions who had the kind of dreams I had long since forgotten about.

The fight against Santemore was even for the first six rounds, and then I began to tire. Santemore worked from a distance and jabbed his way to a decision win. Maybe it was time to devote myself full-time to my janitorial business after all.

Two weeks after dropping the decision to Santemore, I returned back to action in the small community of Wales, Wisconsin, located about an hour west of Milwaukee. The ring was set up in a field near a tavern called Max's Place. The last time I had fought outdoors was on the undercard of Ali-Norton III at Yankee Stadium, and this wasn't quite the same thing.

A standard boxing ring measures between 20 and 24 feet, but since there were no other boxing rings then available in Wisconsin, the promoter had settled for the next best thing, a 17-foot professional wrestling ring. Actually, I wish all my bouts had taken place in a ring that small. Not even Holmes or Ali could've stayed away from me then.

At one end of the field in Wales stood a huge inflated beer can. Situated near the ring was a beer tent and a concession stand serving the official state meal: bratwurst and roasted corn. During the singing of the national anthem, a few over-served spectators yelled "Take it off!" to the attractive young vocalist. Not exactly a black-tie affair at Caesar's Palace, but it was a paycheck.

The crowd at this Sunday afternoon event downed beer and prayed that the dark clouds hanging overhead wouldn't produce a big rainstorm and deprive them of the opportunity to enjoy a little bloodshed with their food. I peeked outside of my dressing room which was located in the basement of the tavern. This was more of a sideshow than a boxing match, and I had done my part to add to the carnival atmosphere.

Earlier in the day, I appeared at the weigh-in in front of a few reporters and several fans. After I jumped off the scale, it was my opponent Chuck Gardner's turn to get weighed. A Minnesota-based club fighter, Gardner had just told the press that he "kind of idolized old Earnie," with an emphasis on "old". The poor guy clearly wasn't expecting what happened next: as he stood there on the scale, I walked right up to him and began eyeballing him up and down, my face lit up with a huge smile as if I was a starving man who'd just had a succulent roast put in front of him. Gardner almost had a childish accident right there.

Unfortunately for him, the rain held off and I didn't. I polished off old Chuck-roast in two, and was given a warm reception by the Wisconsin fans. I enjoyed the Badger State's form of hospitality and hung around for a few hours signing autographs and posing for pictures in back of the tavern before returning to Virginia to concentrate on my janitorial service.

I had again announced my retirement from boxing, but fight offers kept pouring in. I figured what the hell, if someone planned to throw a suitcase full of money my way, I was open for offers any day of the week. There were so few recognizable names in the heavyweight division that even a golden oldie like me could still generate interest. When promoter Ron Weathers presented me with a three-fight package deal, with the first bout in El Paso, Texas, on November 5, 1982, I figured why not.

My opponent was Tony Perea, a football coach at nearby Bowie High School. Perea was 13-0 when he entered the ring to deafening noise from the crowd of 4,000+ at the El Paso Civic Center.

In the opening minute of the bout, I connected with an overhand right that cut Perea's right eyelid. Soon, every time I connected with a punch people in the crowd let loose with boos. I clinched a few times when Perea attacked with wild onrushes. There were boos then, too. I wasn't used to playing the villain, even in the other guy's backyard. Perea rallied in the second round and the crowd cheered wildly. But blood from his cut soon speckled the referee and the canvas. The ref let the bout continue until after the sixth round, when Perea's cornermen called off the match before the seventh started. Perea wept openly in his corner. The pain of losing his first contest before family, friends, and students probably was worse than the cut.

I told him to hang in there, and said that with the right training and proper matchmaking he could still make some money in boxing. But I never heard anything of him again.

"Not bad for an old man," I joked to the press. In reality, I was just there for the payday. I had been in the gym about 10 days in the last four months. My motto: "Have gloves, will travel."

The idea was for me to fight contender George Chaplin in El Paso if I got by Robin Griffin next, but Griffin didn't have the fan base Perea had, and only 900 spectators attended the bout. Griffin was a tall, lanky kid who didn't want to mix it up with me. For the first few rounds he flat-out ran. I paced myself because I had spent the previous weeks running my janitorial business instead of preparing for the fight. After 10 dull rounds I got the decision.

Afterward, Weathers told me the Chaplin fight was temporarily on hold. Weathers felt that without a strong local drawing card, a Shavers-Chaplin bout wouldn't sell as many tickets in El Paso as he had originally thought.

Once again it looked like my fighting days were over. But now I knew better than to count on it.

"I'm through with the fight game—but don't print that," I told Bruce Williams of the *El Paso Herald-Post*. "I may come out of retirement next week."

Sure enough, Weathers made the Chaplin fight in Baltimore, Chaplin's hometown. You'd think the local hero would want to wow his fans by riding into battle with guns blazing, but Chaplin was afraid of me and purposely tied me up the entire fight. I got so frustrated by his antics that I threw an intentional blow south of the border and was immediately disqualified by the referee in the ninth round.

It was definitely time to reenter the 9-5 life. "I've been on the road for 13 years," I told Ralph Wiley of *Sports Illustrated*. "I'm tired. The man ended up with the money, and I ended up with the headaches and the Epson salts. It's a cold-hearted business, where out of 23 people, 22 are thieves. I was too nice."

No punch ever hit me harder than the death of my mother on October 16, 1983. Lung cancer was the cause. She had never smoked a day in her life, but Dad was a three-pack-a-day man, and so she was inhaling that poison right along with him. I've heard statistics that something like 53,000 people a year die of lung cancer from breathing in second-hand smoke.

What got me was that she worked hard her entire life and got sick before she could enjoy retirement. I had made plans for Mom to retire and wanted her to start doing some nice things like traveling and seeing the world. She was always so unassuming. She saved, saved, and saved for a new home, but never had the chance to enjoy it. La Verne and I gave her tons of money over the years, and she would never spend it. She was a child of the Great Depression and was always afraid of going broke.

What I learned from my mother was to enjoy life to the fullest, and to save for your retirement. Unfortunately, I only practiced her advice on saving once I reached middle age. She took one trip her entire life, and that was to visit her family back in Alabama. Mom could have gone on family trips around the world with me, La Verne, and the kids, but she didn't want me to spend the money on her. She was completely unselfish and preferred we use the money for our children.

My mother was the most loyal and admirable person I ever knew. For many years, my siblings and I tried to talk her into leaving our father, because he was never as good to her as she deserved. But she had given her word to God when they married, and to her that was an unbreakable contract.

"I got married in a Church of God, and because he's my husband, I'm committed to him," Mom said. "I'm married to him for life."

I was at Mom's bedside when she passed. Her last words to me were, "Take good care of La Verne." Mom was so happy I married her. They were very close and even prayed together on the phone. If my mother had lived, I doubt La Verne and I would have ever separated, because Mom wouldn't have allowed it

The things my mother taught me have been invaluable to me over the course of my lifetime and continue to change me as I embrace her wise teachings and memorable examples of how she lived her life. I look back now and marvel at the way she raised us. My entire family lived well because of my mother's teachings. She taught us to love everyone, and that when we got hired for a job, our responsibility was to give 110 percent.

"If you do a good job, your employer will tell a few people," she told us. "If you do a bad job, they'll tell everyone." My mother wasn't a very educated woman, but she got her smarts and common sense from the Bible. I thank God for her every day, and I still miss her.

Things were bad all around on the home front. Knock Out Janitorial Supply Inc. went down for the count. I had spent a lot of time on the road and in training camps during the two years that I owned the business, trying to find that last big payday in the ring. I should have kept a better eye on the books.

Jimmy Adams was a better talker than he was a manager of my company, and under his direction, things went steadily south. I was fortunate enough, though, to sell my company and its clients to two local women who ran their own maid service. Last I heard, the business was doing well.

After my association with Adams ended, he left the sport of boxing for several years. But later Jimmy turned around and made Martinsville into a haven for Don King's come-backing heavyweights.

Over the years, fighters such as Bert Cooper, James Tillis, and Oliver McCall eventually made Martinsville their home. Adams was in Cooper's corner the night he almost upset Evander Holyfield in 1991.

Things didn't pan out so well for the emotionally troubled McCall, who went into a rage and flipped out in Martinsville.

As for me, as long as I remained a man of integrity and was true to my word, I knew it would open doors for me. But I put my foot down when La Verne suggested that I take a job in a local factory. I had been through too much to go back.

"Those days are over, honey," I told her.

Not long after that, so was my marriage. It pains me to this day to say it, but I never really was in love with La Verne. I loved her for who she was, but I was never truly, madly, passionately in love with her. She was and still is a great lady, but I married her because I thought she would be a great mother for my children, not because I was head over heels in love.

The hardest words I've ever said in my life were when I told my wife of almost 20 years that I didn't want to be married to her anymore. It was painful to say it, and I'm sure for La Verne, it was 10 times as hard hearing it.

"Earnie, I know you have never loved me, but you have always been so good to me and the kids," La Verne admitted. It broke my heart to hear those words because La Verne loved me unconditionally. She was the backbone of our family and the perfect wife. I had been far from the world's greatest husband, but we had raised five beautiful daughters and had come through a lot of rough times. However, I had given in to temptation too many times, and now I was too selfish to realize what I was throwing away. La Verne was all the woman I needed, but I couldn't see it at the time. Divorcing her and breaking up my family has been the single greatest regret of my life. It hurt my daughters that I no longer wanted to be with their mother, but they were wonderful through it all and didn't take sides.

The pain of divorce lasts for years, but even worse is when children are forced to endure the pain of coming from a broken home. They carry that with them in some form for the rest of their lives, and it isn't fair.

Of course the divorce was bound to put another large dent in my wallet. When we arrived in divorce court, I was pleasantly surprised to find out the judge was a black man. I thought, "This brother ought to be able to relate to another black man. He'll go easy on me."

I strutted into the courtroom with a cheesy smile on my face, pronounced rhythm in my step, and opened the proceedings with a fraternal display of ebonics.

"Hey, your honor, what it be like?" I said to my judicial brother, flashing him my friendliest smile.

"Not like you, Mr. Shavers," the judge shot back, glaring at me. Clearly, this was going to cost me. After the judge heard both sides, he handed down his ruling. To divorce La Verne would cost me $1 million in alimony.

When I heard that figure, I shot up out of my chair with an objection right out of a bad episode of *Perry Mason*.

"But your honor, I love this woman!"

The judge was nonplused, and sat there for a second.

"When did you finally figure out you loved this woman, Mr. Shavers?" he asked.

"When you said it was going to cost me $1 million," I said. Everybody laughed but me.

But once again La Verne came to my rescue. Have you ever heard of a wife voluntarily taking less alimony from her husband, especially when she has earned every penny? That's what La Verne did. She was incredible about the whole thing.

It was time for a fresh start. I enjoyed living in Martinsville, but it was too small for both of us to live there after our divorce. She wanted to stay, preferring not to uproot our daughters again. They had made new friends in the three years since we moved there and were happy in Virginia.

I moved back to Warren In 1984. It was someplace familiar, and besides, I wanted to be near Veronica and my daughter Lisa. Next to La Verne, Veronica was the best woman I knew, and I was still infatuated with her beauty. Veronica was low maintenance, too. She never asked for anything and never pressured me to do anything.

"See you when I see you," she'd always say. Well, I would be seeing Veronica real soon.

CHAPTER SEVENTEEN

On the Comeback Trail

After I went back to Warren, I was offered a job by a friend in Youngstown selling meat products door-to-door. He figured because everyone in the area knew me, I'd be a natural salesman and people would want to buy any product I was associated with.

The idea of selling meat products was intriguing to me, but having a person to answer to was not. I decided to go into the door-to-door meat market on my own, using my own company title, "Earnie Shavers Home Delivery Meat Products." I sold high-quality meat at affordable prices. With my work ethic I figured I could turn this operation into a real cash cow. I decided that I would take my business where no man had taken it before: the ghetto. The way I had it figured, the people there love to eat, and they could pay with their food stamps. One thing about people in the ghetto—they eat very well.

I couldn't afford a porterhouse steak every night, but the people in the 'hood could. They bought the best cuts of meats—Porterhouse steaks, ribeye steaks, T-bones, filet mignon, and even lobster. I had never eaten a lobster in my life. I admired their champagne-and-caviar tastes. Don't ever let it be said that people in the ghetto don't have good taste. But what definitely can be said is that a lot of them will go out of their way to avoid paying their bills.

My honeymoon with the 'hood was over when I heard, "Earnie, I'm a little short this week, can you cut me a break and I'll catch up with you next week?" I forgot the golden rule: once they've eaten the meat, they damn sure aren't going to pay for it. As soon as I let one customer have a break, it was as if the cat was out of the bag. In record time the rest of my clients began asking for credit. I heard all the lame excuses and sob stories, too.

'Earnie, I'll pay you on Friday, man." Come Friday, the person was a ghost.

"Earnie, my old man up and left me and I need to feed my kids." I'd eventually find out there never was an old man, nor even kids, for that matter.

"Earnie, they're going to shut off my electricity if I don't pay my bill this week." Then I'd find out the electricity had been shut off months before.

"Earnie, my mother died and I used the meat money to pay for her funeral expenses." Must have been a pretty cheap funeral.

As if all that wasn't bad enough, my clients began moving on me. They'd think nothing of moving in the middle of the night because they owed someone money. Just uproot their whole family to keep one step ahead of the bill collectors. It was unbelievable.

I ended up spending more time, gas, and wear and tear on my vehicles trying to get money from them than I did delivering meat. Finally, I decided it was time to get an assistant, someone whose no-nonsense attitude would strike instant fear in the hearts of anyone trying to cheat me out of what was rightfully mine. His name was Smith & Wesson. But packing heat brought its own set of problems I soon found out—because I wasn't the only one doing it.

I'll never forget one of my best customers, a 350-pound woman who was known as "Sweet Pea." Initially, it was love at first sight: I had the meat and Sweet Pea had the killer appetite and government-issued food stamps. It was a match made in heaven. The woman practically could have opened a deli in her apartment, she had so much meat in her refrigerator and freezer. But in due time, she couldn't or wouldn't pay her meat bill, either. Heartache for me, and empty stomach for her.

"Sorry, Sweet Pea, but I can't keep giving you credit if you don't make any sort of attempt to pay off your bill," I said politely when I bumped into her in the parking lot of her apartment complex.

Sweet Pea didn't like that and expressed her disapproval by whipping out a pistol and emptying its contents in my direction. Luckily for me, she missed. Then it was my turn. I took out my gun and returned fire. All 350 pounds of her ran the 100-yard dash up into her apartment in record time. That ol' gal had some flab on her body, but she had some serious wheels, too.

In dealing with ghetto folks I came to understand there was an entirely different mentality going on with them. They were always bitching and moaning about how the white man kept messing with their welfare checks.

"Damn, bro, the white man just keeps fucking up my shit," I heard one brother say. I decided to engage him on this point to see where he was coming from. Left field, it turned out.

"How do you figure it's the white man?" I asked. "You don't even work! You're on welfare."

"Well, the white man is always trying to screw with my checks," he said. All I could do was shake my big bald head and try to give him a gentle nudge in the direction of the real world.

"I know many white businessmen," I told him, "and they don't sit at work behind their computer terminals trying to figure out how to block you from getting your welfare check."

My entire life, many white businessmen had opened doors for me and offered me a hand up. That's how I made it. Many of the people I met in the ghetto didn't care about the future—theirs or anybody else's. They were only interested in getting something for nothing, and when it wasn't enough they played the blame game. It was everybody's fault but their own. They weren't interested in work, and they sure weren't interested in coughing up the $7,500 they owed me for my meat.

I hate to sound like one of those smug, rich, white politicians always yapping about those no-good lazy welfare people, but the fact is that those no-good lazy welfare people ended up putting me out of business. Looking back it's kind of ironic: it was much easier getting money out of heroin dealers, degenerate gamblers, and junkies than it was to get money out of welfare people in the ghetto. Finally, I just shut my business down for good. Let them eat cake!

Two weeks later, a familiar name came to my rescue. The name was King, but the call I received in early 1985 was from Mrs. Henrietta King, Don's wife. She wondered if I was interested in coming to work for her as the director of her husband's training camp. I was at first a little skeptical, given the fact that the man she had vowed to love, honor, and obey made some of my former meat clients look like paragons of virtue. But Mrs. King was nobody's fool.

"Earnie, I know Don wasn't fair to you in your business dealings," she said, "but he's my husband, and I have to support him. If you come to work for me, I'll pay you what you want."

I'd briefly worked for Mrs. King in 1974 as a handyman, gardener, and chauffeur. Unlike other members of her family, if you gave her an honest day's work, you couldn't ask for a better person to work for. She was a wonderful lady.

"I'll take the job," I told her, "but Don King can never go over my head. I cannot be an effective camp director if everyone goes to Don when they have a problem with me."

She agreed to my terms, and offered a base salary of $3,000 a week, plus free room and board at the camp. It was a done deal.

Veronica was living in Youngstown, and I saw her once a week, mostly to bring home my paycheck. After she saw the zeros on my first paycheck from Henrietta King, Veronica was as enthusiastic about the arrangement as I was. It was one of the greatest jobs I've ever had. I learned so much from Mrs. King, and she taught me how to be a better businessperson.

"Earnie, whenever you attempt to sell anything, let the other person quote you a price first," she said. Mrs. King also taught me the fine art of buying real estate, saying if I really wanted to buy land I should approach the seller directly rather than go through an agent and cut out their percentage. I took her advice and bought a parcel in Leavittsburg, Ohio, putting 10 percent down.

Meanwhile, in Don King land I ran things the way I thought best. King wanted successful fighters and contenders, and he expected me to get them into top fighting form. I knew exactly what a fighter had to do to win and have some longevity in the fight game. I generally had very little trouble with the fighters, but every now and then I did have my authority challenged by a young pup who thought the old bull wasn't what he used to be.

One was heavyweight Mitch "Blood" Green, a wild kid from New York who might have developed into something if he'd used his head for something besides target practice for the other guy's fists. When I arrived at camp I learned that Green had virtually terrorized everyone there for a whole year with his ghetto ways. That wouldn't fly anymore—there was a new sheriff in town. I went to Green's room, locked the door behind me, and laid down the law.

"Mitch, we got rules this year, and they're real simple," I started off. "No women allowed in camp. Curfew is 10 p.m. sharp. Now, if you don't like it, one of two things can happen: you can kick my ass, or I can kick your ass. But if I win, you'll have to leave. I'll take your contract and put it on a shelf for three years."

Green's reaction wasn't unexpected.

"Oh, man ... fuck this shit, man. I'm getting out of here," he said. He didn't run back to his own hood, of course, but straight to Don King. To his credit, Don told Green to either shape up or ship out.

To Green's credit, after King told him who was boss, he came back with his tail between his legs and apologized. He turned out to be my best buddy in camp.

"Earnie, you're a good brother, man," Mitch said. "Any time you come to New York, you call me and I'll hook you up."

"I appreciate the invitation, Mitch, but I ain't calling you, so let's get that straight right now," I said as diplomatically as I could. Green hailed from the meanest streets of New York, and I didn't foresee a time when I'd be in his neighborhood, unless I planned on becoming a Mack Daddy, slumlord, or crack addict. But as long as we stayed on safe Buckeye turf, we were cool.

Another problem child in camp at first was Tim Witherspoon. Witherspoon had briefly held the WBC heavyweight championship, and made it clear the rules applied only to mere mortals, which left him out. I told Tim the same thing I told Green, and it went in one ear and out the other. That same night he went out on the town and stayed out way past curfew. When he came back the next morning, I told him to take his ex-heavyweight championship fat ass back to Philadelphia.

"Tim, pack your shit, man, you're out of here," I said.

"What?" he said, acting all innocent. He was now Mr. Babe in the Woods, acting as if he didn't have a clue.

"Pack your shit. You're outta here," I repeated. Witherspoon called Don, who told him he needed to work things out with me if he wanted to stay in camp. No dummy, he knew what he had to do: tuck his tail between his legs and crawl back into the dog house. When Tim returned, he was a spoon dipped in honey.

"Earnie, I'm sorry, man. I'm really sorry. I made a mistake," he said timidly.

"Damn right you made a mistake!" I said very untimidly.

"Earnie, I really love you, man. You cool," he said.

"Tim, this is for your own good," I said. "Now drop and give me 100 pushups."

Witherspoon was putty in my hands from that day on. I told all the guys in the camp the same thing: I wasn't there to be their friend, or play wet nurse to any of them. If I didn't get those guys in tip-top condition, it was my job on the line, not theirs. I had a camp to run, and I grew to like my six-figure salary. Don King later paid me the highest compliment concerning my strictly business attitude.

"Man, Earnie, all these guys in camp don't like you, but they respect you," he said. That's all I really ever cared about.

Although I had a good, steady paycheck and the regular companionship of Veronica, I was still experiencing a personal emptiness and void in my life. Then suddenly Veronica wanted to get married, and my whole life was about to change—for better, as they say, and for worse.

CHAPTER EIGHTEEN

Saved by the Bell

While working at the Kings' camp, I started to attend a small church in Orwell, Ohio. Paula Johnson, one of my few reliable customers from my meat-selling days, invited me to attend. Paula was not only a good paying customer, but was also an attractive, cheerful, friendly person. I noticed she always had a smile on her face. One day I finally just had to ask her why she was so happy all the time.

"It's because I have Jesus Christ in my heart, Earnie," she said. Oh boy, I thought, cringing inside, I've got a real live one on my hands. In the past, whenever anyone mentioned they were a born-again Christian, my knee-jerk reaction was to grab my wallet and tip-toe in the opposite direction.

The difference this time was that the person saying it had the kind of shape that would make the Angel Gabriel put down his horn. I'll be honest, I wanted to get to know her in more than just the biblical sense. So I was delighted when she invited me to go with her one night to a spiritual nightclub in Cleveland. That's right, a spiritual nightclub.

The establishment had been a regular nightclub before the owner had a dramatic, life-changing experience. After his wife was killed in an accident, he became a born-again Christian and turned his bar into a spiritual nightclub. It featured Christian music and choirs, and a Christian comic who emceed the nightly entertainment. No alcohol was served, no smoking was allowed, and there was no cover charge. The whole place ran strictly on donations. I ended up enjoying everything so much I left a $50 bill in the donation box at the end of the night. This place just blew my mind.

A few days later, Paula invited me to a church in Warren to see her brother-in-law preach. I'd known Richard Oliver when he was a musician in a successful rock band in the area. Then he got saved by God, and for five years had been the pastor of the church Paula took me to that Sunday. Looking back, it was obvious that it was God's hand, not Paula's, leading me there.

As Reverend Oliver preached, it was as if his message went directly to my soul. He told about how successful he was as a musician, touring all around the world and how adored he was by total strangers. He said he could buy anything he wanted—cars, designer clothes, beautiful women, drugs—but discovered he still had an emptiness deep down inside that worldly, material possessions and adoration just could not fill.

Then he decided to turn to Jesus, and all he'd been missing was found. He never looked back.

"Money can buy your admission to any place in the world but Heaven," Oliver preached. "Only Jesus Christ can fill your heart with happiness."

His message changed my entire life in the blink of an eye. The date was April 24, 1986. Now when I recall my old lifestyle, I nervously chuckle thinking about how money was my God. That's how the real one got my attention. God allowed me to lose everything I owned. I lost the mansion, all the money in every bank account, my wife, and all the other women. The women for the most part actually left on their own when they found out all my money was gone. I had lived the lifestyle of the rich and famous, but I was still empty inside.

But my salvation was far more important than any of the material possessions I had acquired in my professional career, including my championship fights against Muhammad Ali and Larry Holmes. Now, while I didn't make the money I had once made boxing for a living, I had something far more precious: complete peace of mind.

I can't tell you how many people come up to me and say, "Earnie, I hear you've found God." I always correct them. "No, God wasn't lost," I say. "I was."

Money and material things can never give you peace of mind. Worldly pleasures are never what they promise to be. I had everything life had to offer, and still it wasn't enough to bring me the happiness I craved. I was still making very good money with Don King, but now I felt a higher calling. If you had told me while I was boxing that one day I would be in the ministry, I would have laughed in your face. Preaching was the furthest thing from my mind.

But now I felt called by God to spread his word where it was needed the most. I decided to go to jails, prisons, halfway homes, youth centers and do the Lord's work by trying to reach souls hardened by hate and lives of deprivation and depravity.

When I accepted Christ into my life, I didn't just talk the talk. I also walked the walk—right out of my home with my long-time lover Veronica and into an apartment. I wanted to live in a Godly way.

Naturally, Veronica put up an ungodly fuss.

"I can't believe you used me like this!" she howled.

She had a point. Veronica had never pressured me, even when I was married to La Verne. She had hoped we'd eventually get married, but never banked on it.

After a lot of back and forth, I proposed a compromise.

"If you become a Christian, I'll marry you," I promised her.

"OK," Veronica said. "I'll get saved."

It was a mistake to force her to become a Christian. Veronica wanted me, not Christ, but I was willing to take her conversion, such as it was, at face value.

We got married in Youngstown in July 1986. There's an old saying about marrying your mistress—when you do, you create a vacancy. Take it from the expert: it's true. Thirty minutes after we got married, I said to myself, "I just made the biggest mistake of my life." Disaster always strikes when you lead with your chin inside the ring, and with your groin outside of it.

Marriage wasn't the only arena in which I tried a comeback. When George Foreman announced in 1987 that he was returning to boxing after 10 years out of the ring, I decided to come out of retirement, too, in hopes of landing a big money fight against him. With all of the cancellations of Foreman-Shavers matches over the years, I felt Big George still owed me a fight. Some of my friends questioned my sanity. I was 42 years old then. But if I could get a few good paydays to help bankroll my burgeoning ministry, it would be worth it.

My boxing comeback began at a technical college in Cincinnati. A sparse crowd of 400 watched me flatten little-known Larry Sims in the second round. It was not a riveting performance. A lot of ring rust had accumulated during my three-year layoff, and my timing was off.

But I was still convinced I had a few good fights left. I didn't feel much different physically than when I was in my prime, and I did miss the roar of the crowd. But my primary motivation was getting a big money shot at Foreman. Or, if not him, then Mike Tyson.

Tyson then ruled the heavyweight division with no visible threat to his supremacy. I thought a fight between a couple of explosive fellows like us could generate some big interest, and frankly the top contenders of the mid-80s seemed a far cry from the breed of cat prowling the division in my time. Even guys who claimed portions of the heavyweight throne in the "me" decade, like Tony Tubbs and Pinklon Thomas, would not have cracked the top 10 in my era. If my old trainer Archie Moore could fight effectively into his 40s, why couldn't I? Sugar Ray Leonard had just shocked the world by returning to boxing after a three-and-a-half-year hiatus to take the middleweight title from Marvin Hagler. A miracle had happened when I was born again spiritually. Who was to say I couldn't engineer another kind as a born-again heavyweight?

I signed to box undefeated prospect Art Card in an exhibition match in Akron. A sold-out crowd at Jackie Lee's Place cheered as I made my way to the ring. It felt good, and just moments after the bell it felt even better when I dumped Card to the canvas with a straight right. But Card bounced up and gave me problems for the rest of the three-round exhibition. It might take a real miracle after all to get me back where I needed to be.

Not long after that I approached Tyson's manager, Jimmy Jacobs, about a fight with the young champion. Jacobs was a straight talker and painted a bleak picture for me of my prospects of ever getting in the ring with the guy *Sports Illustrated* called "Kid Dynamite."

"You're a puncher, Earnie, and that makes you dangerous," Jacobs said. "Mike is in a no-win situation: If you beat him, they'll say he's washed up, and if he beats you, they'll call it an unimpressive win over an old boxer. He can't win either way."

Jacobs was only doing what a good manager should do—protecting his boxer's career. Be that as it may, I think that a lot of boxers from my era would have beaten Mike Tyson. As a fighter, he had no heart. A fighter with heart could beat him, as Buster Douglas and Evander Holyfield later proved. With his scowl and ghetto talk, Tyson put the fear of God in many of his opponents, and that's half the battle. But when you bullied him right back, and followed it up with four or five punch combinations, you owned him. Tyson's career was as good as over once Cus D'Amato and Jacobs died. When Don King stepped into the picture, Tyson's head got messed up but good.

Although we never met in the ring, I did get the opportunity to meet him in another challenging venue after Tyson was sent to prison for the rape of Desiree Washington. I went there to visit him and we had a pleasant conversation. I explained to Mike some of the difficulties that accompany fame, how when you're in the public spotlight, you're on a platform whether you like it or not.

"You need to start acting like a man and be responsible for your actions, or you end up in a place like this," I told him. "There is a void in your life that can't be filled with anything in the world. It has to be filled by God." Mike listened attentively, but I don't know if the words sank in. It's impossible to have a positive impact on everyone no matter how hard you try.

My former trainer, Frank Luca, had moved to Arizona, and he invited me down for a look around. I liked what I saw and moved to Phoenix later that same year. For three months I worked on salary in public relations for a land developer. Then I was called into the full-time ministry by Pastor Tommy Barnett at the Phoenix First Assembly Church on Cave Creek Road.

Pastor Barnett got me speaking engagements at area churches for $500 an appearance. I was an evangelist for the Lord, a calling I felt in the depths of my soul. Pretty soon I was getting $1,000 a night. Then I switched over to strictly donations, or what they call in the ministry "love offerings." My first night out, I made $1,500.

Pastor Barnett warned me that the ministry was no different than other professions in that it has its share of crooks and con men. He told me who were crooks, who to watch out for, and who to collect money from up-front before a speaking engagement. I eventually got $2,000 a night, and all the doors started opening up. My whole life changed as a result of giving everything to the Lord.

While my professional life was a slice of heaven, my home life was downright hell. My new career didn't go over well with Veronica. The days of "I'll see you when I see you" were long over. Now Veronica didn't like it when I was on the road all the time. She became bored and occupied herself reading scandalous tabloids and watching soap operas, neither of which preached a good, righteous lifestyle. I could feel her hostility as soon as I walked into the house after an evangelical road trip.

Most of those road trips took me to prisons. I believed that was God's personal mission for me because I connected so effortlessly with these incarcerated men. Being a professional boxer, I won their instant respect. That and the fact that I took out time in my schedule to spend time with them touched their hearts, and gave me the opportunity to share my life with them.

At one time, I could have easily been in their shoes. I told them I had made some wrong choices, including the people I'd once hung out with and the adulterous lifestyle I had lived. I preached that money never brought me security or happiness. I was once rich and famous, I had a mansion, limousine, nice clothes, plenty of money, and absolutely zero peace of mind.

After I'd gone over my background, I'd put the question of eternity in their minds.

"Do you know when you're going to die?" I'd ask. Of course they didn't.

Then I'd ask them if they were to die tonight, where they would spend eternity? Even the toughest cons blinked hard at that one, and more than a few ended up on their knees with me.

I often told the story of the man I'd met in Connecticut. As I was in this church preaching, this white guy walked in, and I knew instantly and without question that I was looking at Satan in the flesh.

He was built like Arnold Schwarzenegger, but the look in his fierce eyes, which locked right on mine, was much more riveting than the muscles. He stood in the corner and kept those burning eyes on me as I made the traditional altar call. That's when you invite people who want to be saved to step forward and receive Jesus Christ. But this guy just stood there giving me the willies. When the service ended he was still there, and I boldly approached him.

"How come you didn't come forward?" I asked.

"My hand moved, but I didn't put it up," he said. "I can't get saved."

Then I put my palm on his forehead and asked Jesus to come into his heart. All of a sudden, this guy started speaking in tongues as the Holy Spirit entered him. Then something even more startling happened. He confessed to me that on the day before he came to church, he was planning to kill a busload of school kids. This guy was in perfect condition and did 1,000 sit-ups a day. He wore a black leather jacket and looked beyond evil—he was diabolical. And he was definitely planning on killing those kids.

"I had the gun ready, the bullets, the whole thing," he said.

After he got off work that Friday, he heard a voice tell him to go get a newspaper. My picture was in it, with a notice about my service. Then he heard another voice tell him to go see me.

I learned that he had served in Vietnam, where he was captured by the enemy. They tried all manner of brutal torture to make him talk, including holding a lighter under his arm. But this strong, hard man refused to break. But it came with a horrible price tag. In the process of making himself impervious to pain, he also made himself impervious to love and other positive emotions. He came back to the States whole on the outside but crippled on the inside. His rampant, all-inclusive hate was the only stimuli to which he responded. He was dead serious about killing these kids on the bus, and had even told his parents of his plan. They couldn't talk him out of it, and I'm sure they were trembling with fear at the prospect of what he was going to do.

When he came to the church service and got saved, it changed everything in his life. He wasn't just saved, but healed, too. He stayed in touch with me through letters and said he stayed in the Word, went to church, and even found a loving wife. He now shares his testimony with anyone who will listen. He shares how God's love changed his heart and life. The man who didn't want anyone to like him was now loved, and loving.

"Earnie, God used you so that he could reach me," he said.

Since then, I've preached to a lot of cold-hearted killers and reached them, and when they get out of prison, they're still on fire for the Lord. There was no doubt the prison ministry was my true calling. I would eventually visit up to 250 prisons and travel more than 300,000 miles a year and get invitations from Cuba, Russia, and Africa.

As much as I preach the word of God, I am known as the "Knockout Evangelist" and sometimes people want to hear more about my punching than my preaching, or just see for themselves if the Acorn is what he was cracked up to be. I remember once in Minneapolis, a blind man was aided to the altar. I embraced him as he came forward, then he asked to feel my right arm. He wrapped both of his hands around my biceps, smiled, and said, "Amen!"

But there was still one person I couldn't seem to reach—my own wife, Veronica. Plain and simple, since I had become a Christian, she no longer trusted me. She accused me of cheating, the way I had cheated on La Verne with her. I was preaching, not cheating, but Veronica's lack of trust engendered so much hostility and bitterness in the house, it grew unbearable.

"Earnie, when you get back, I'll be gone," she said as I prepared for another road trip. She went back to Ohio and we divorced in early 1990. I can't say I was too upset, because in the back of my mind I felt Veronica had forced me to marry her, and under false pretenses at that. She'd never really accepted the Lord, nor my vocation.

I stayed in touch with her, keeping tabs on Lisa and sending the proper support money to see she had everything she needed. What I didn't do was put my heart on the shelf for a while. Some men collect coins, others collect cars. I just happened to collect wives. Not that I ever intended to be married five times; things just sort of happened.

Shortly after Veronica left me, I met a lady named Hazel Barnes at church. Hazel was a receptionist who worked in a satellite office for Trinity Broadcasting in Phoenix. Beautiful, friendly, a solid Christian lady, she seemed an ideal prospect for the next Mrs. Shavers. Did I mention beautiful?

On top of all that, Hazel didn't long to have her own career and actually liked the idea of keeping the home fires burning while I was out on the road. Never one to waste a lot of time, we married in 1990, not long after I was granted a divorce from Veronica. We enjoyed three good years together while I was in the ministry. Then we had our first and last big blowout.

My daughter Lisa, now 13 and a typical teenager, was going through a rebellious phase at home and wasn't getting along with her mother, Veronica, back in Columbus, Ohio. What she needed was a little discipline and a lot of her father.

"My daughter Lisa is coming to live with us for a while," I said to Hazel, expecting her full acquiescence. But instead my wife crossed her arms and delivered her own pronouncement.

"She can't come," Hazel said. That really threw me for a loop, and I asked her for an explanation.

"All my kids are grown up, and I don't want any more children around," Hazel said. That was understandable, I guess, and I couldn't argue with her. However, the bottom line was that my daughter needed me, she was my blood, and my house was her house, which is what I told Hazel. But she was obstinate, telling me, "If your daughter comes to live in our home, I'm leaving."

I was just as obstinate. "If you don't want my daughter," I told her, "then you don't want me." Which is how it turned out. Wife #3 packed up and departed for good.

So unlucky at love was I. Hazel's sudden departure was a sucker punch that knocked the wind out of me and left a large hole in my life. If I was going to be taking shots like that, I figured I might as well get paid for it.

On a ministry trip in Florida shortly after Hazel's departure, I received the news that an ancient George Foreman had shocked the world by regaining the heavyweight title, knocking out Michael Moorer. It was enough to get an old fellow thinking.

Through the years, many big-name boxers, including Joe Louis, Muhammad Ali, and Sugar Ray Leonard, had returned to the ring after announcing their retirements. Boxers, more than any athletes, led the list of returning retirees in sports.

When a big-name boxer retires, it is always followed by a question mark, because you never know how long it will last. Of all the heavyweight champions, only Gene Tunney and Rocky Marciano went out on top and stayed retired. There had been celebrated comebacks in other sports, of course—Gordie Howe made a hockey comeback in his fifties, Mark Spitz tried to recapture Olympic glory, Magic Johnson attempted a basketball return, Jim Palmer wanted to see if he still had any juice behind his fast ball, Bjorn Borg gave his tennis racket another swing, and Michael Jordan stepped back onto the basketball court in October 2001 sporting a Washington Wizards uniform.

But the most amazing comeback of all time had to be Foreman's miraculous return to the heavyweight throne. That he recaptured the title almost 20 years after losing it was amazing. And to Foreman it was worth millions in and out of the ring.

Boxing is one of the few sports that welcomes back its retirees even though they're far from what they used to be. In team sports, an athlete's comeback usually ends because he can no longer earn a spot on the roster. But because a boxer's marketability is as important as his ability to hook off the jab, a big-name fighter can usually find himself a promoter willing to take a chance on him again. As for the boxers themselves, some miss the glory, while others need the money. Some just don't know what to do with themselves or how to replace the natural high they get from hard physical competition. For me, the simple answer was dollars and cents. A fight with Foreman would financially set me and my ministry up for life.

I was almost 50 years old, even older than Foreman. Of course many thought I was crazy to even think about getting back in the ring, but the same had once been said about Foreman. No one was laughing at him once he regained the world title.

Ron Weathers had promoted two of my fights in El Paso, Texas. Now Foreman's business manager, Weathers had masterfully plotted Big George's campaign to regain the title. I called him and he immediately agreed to chart my comeback, too. Weathers ran a training camp in New Mexico, and that's where I headed to start the process of scraping off eight years' worth of ring rust.

Weather's camp was in Ruidoso, in the mountains. It was quickly apparent that getting back into fighting shape would be no piece of cake. I still had my power, but my timing and reflexes were missing.

The first four months in camp were pretty brutal on this old man, and it was harder than ever before. But hard work never bothered me, and I was determined to keep at it.

There were some decent heavyweights in camp like fringe contenders James Thunder and Tim Puller, and I had difficulty in my initial sparring sessions with them. I'd see an opening, but before I could take advantage of it, my sparring partners were someplace else.

The next 12 months were no picnic, but I got myself in shape and finally was ready to show the public what I could do. It was time for this punching preacher to hit the road again. Only now the ring was my bully pulpit.

CHAPTER NINETEEN

Jolly Ol' England

On September 19,1995, I squared off against Brian Morgan in Omaha, Nebraska. It was a long way from Madison Square Garden, and Morgan was no Muhammad Ali. He had been defeated by fringe contenders Vaughn Bean and Tony La Rosa, and his few victories were over anonymous boxers like Ray Ripping and Jonathan Littles. But he was alive and breathing, and as I recall, that could barely be said of some of the bodies bowled over by Foreman in his comeback. In fact, when reporters would say that one of his opponents must have been taken off a ventilator to fight Big George, Foreman would indignantly reply, tongue in cheek, that only guys who'd been off a ventilator for at least five days were considered as opponents.

Morgan caused me few problems and he had a good chin. I outpointed him in eight rounds in sluggish fashion. It was a baby step in the right direction.

After the fight, I returned to Ruidoso to resume training. At age 50, I didn't have any time to waste. While in Ruidoso, I was introduced to a successful businessman named Doyle Harden, from El Paso, Texas. Harden ran a multimillion dollar import/export company. He and I hit it off, and Harden hired me to do public relations for his company. Then he did something else that would change my life forever.

"Earnie, I'm going to pay you well for your work, but I'm also going to teach you my business and how to save for your retirement," Harden said. He had followed my career, and was aware of my past financial problems. I was all ears.

Harden taught me financial planning wasn't that hard, but it did require some discipline. He told me to put away a certain percentage of my paycheck in an Individual Retirement Account and let the interest compound over a period of years. Compound interest, Harden said, was the eighth wonder of the world.

"Once it compounds, it adds up quickly," Harden said. "Use a small portion to live off of and you'll never go broke again."

Doyle was right. I watched my account grow slowly over time, then it started to compound. Today, I'm financially secure, and I won't ever have to worry about going broke again. I've learned the hard way that it takes more than hard work to put money in the bank. It takes business sense, and Doyle was the best mentor I could have had. I can't thank him and his wonderful family enough for the great times they showed me. He's always been a true gentleman and friend, and my life is so much better for knowing him.

I wish I could say the same about Mr. Brian Yates. He was my second opponent on the comeback trail that was supposed to lead me to a gazillion-dollar payday with Foreman. At least that's what I thought when I took the bout at the Ho-Chunk Casino in Baraboo, Wisconsin. But then I learned in training camp that George had no interest in a match with me, no matter how many guys I beat in my comeback.

As soon as I found that out, my interest in continuing boxing went south.

I'd have retired on the spot, but I was contractually obligated to fight Yates in Wisconsin on November 24, 1995. Oh, well. Yates had a record of 2-12. How tough could he be?

One of the promoters even told a reporter it was intended as "entertainment," not a fight, because on paper it looked like such an obvious mismatch.

Somebody should have told the Wisconsin Department of Regulation and Licensing, the agency that regulates boxing in the Badger State. Out of the blue, the DRL announced that it would not permit me to fight Yates unless it received medical confirmation that my surgically repaired left eye—the one that suffered the detached retina in the second Holmes fight—was ship-shape. Two things about that were funny. Just five years before, the DRL had allowed former junior welterweight champion Aaron Pryor to fight in Madison even after examinations in other states where Pryor had applied for a license to box indicated that Pryor was legally blind in one eye. But the Wisconsin bureaucrats passed him anyway because they didn't want to be accused of discriminating against the handicapped.

The other funny thing about the DRL's sudden concern about my left eye was that in 1982, when I fought Chuck Gardner in Wales, the very same regulatory agency didn't raise an eyebrow about the eye that had been fixed just a couple of years earlier. But now, 13 years and 17 fights later, the eye was a problem?

When a Milwaukee reporter called me long distance in New Mexico to inquire about the eye, I had a ready answer for him: I told him to hold up some fingers for me to count. The DRL preferred something a little more concrete, and after I passed an ophthalmologist's depth-perception test, the fight was approved.

Just my luck.

When I entered the ring at the Ho-Chunk Casino in Baraboo I noticed a familiar face. Dick Bartman, the same guy who'd refereed my fight 14 years earlier against Gardner, was also the referee of this bout. Good thing he looked healthy, because I had a feeling he might have been the only referee the state had.

One-and-a-half rounds later, the unhealthiest-looking guy in the ring was me. Yates, whose nickname was "B-52," bombed me out of boxing for good, knocking me down with right hands until Bartman stopped it. Twenty-five years earlier, the breeze from one of my missed punches would've taken a guy like Yates out. I didn't need a mountain to fall on me, or in this case, a B-52. Getting taken out by Yates was enough to convince me that after 88 professional fights I was done with boxing once and for all.

It was a career that I had no reason to be ashamed of. My only regret was never getting a bout with Big George. A few years later, when we saw each other at the International Boxing Hall of Fame in Canastota, New York, George was typically gracious. When I said I was sorry we'd never crossed gloves, Foreman smiled that cheeseburger pitchman's smile and said, "Earnie, you would've killed me." No wonder he sells so many of those grills.

I may have finally said goodbye to boxing, but not long after that I said hello to wife number four. Her name was Cynthia

Wilmoth, and we met on a flight from Atlanta to Phoenix on April 3, 1993. Cynthia was a flight attendant for America West Airlines. At a slender 5'6" tall, with brown eyes and auburn hair, Cynthia was a prime catch. She sat next to me on the flight and not only did she know I was a boxer, but she had heard of my prison ministry through Meadowlark Lemon, the ex-Harlem Globetrotter and a good friend with whom I did some occasional ministry work.

Cynthia also lived in Phoenix, and we dated a few months before marrying on August 31, 1993. The problem was that when I married Cynthia, I discovered to my dismay that I had also married Cynthia's mother.

Remember when Mike Tyson married actress Robin Givens, how Tyson not only got Givens, but her mother, too? I got the same kind of package deal. Cynthia's mother was always interfering with our lives. She was a very domineering woman who didn't think twice about telling Cynthia, a grown woman, what to do with her life. She treated her daughter like a little child, and Cynthia suffered from having very little self-esteem as a result. Unfortunately, Cynthia never seemed very interested in getting out from under her mother's thumb, and continually sought her approval over mine. It grated on my nerves over time, and after two years, I told Cynthia and her mother we were through. The three of us divorced in July 1996.

Deciding I needed to make a clean break, I moved to Aurora, Colorado. I had done some previous ministry work there, and I thought the fresh air, nice people, and the majestic beauty of the Rocky Mountains made it the perfect place to put down roots.

Once word got around I was living in Aurora, Bill Hardney, a guy I'd KO'd in one round in 1971, who lived nearby, called me up and we got together. He introduced me to Lynette Broadway, who mesmerized me from the get-go. She was a dead-ringer for Veronica, and I was ready for love once again. Eventually, I went to Omaha to meet Lynette's family, and I really hit it off with them.

Lynette and I married on December 31, 1996, in spite of misgivings about Lynette expressed by my daughter, Carla, who said, "Dad, don't spend any more on this wedding, because I don't feel it's going to last very long. You don't know this woman." Her womanly instincts were right on the mark. It wasn't the first time I married for the wrong reasons. Since La Verne and I split up, I'd tried to fill the void by marrying women I'd been only physically attracted to.

It wasn't long before I discovered Lynette was cheating on me. At first, she denied being unfaithful until I told her that I had proof. She finally admitted that she was lonely and I had been gone frequently doing ministry work.

When it came to rationalizations, Lynette was a world champion. "Darling, all the times I slept with him you were on my mind," she said, as if that would make me feel better. "I was wishing it was you, darling. Can you ever forgive me? I still love you."

I wasn't going to give in, but then she hit me where I lived.

"Sweetheart, God said that we must forgive or He won't forgive us. Do you forgive me?" Since I preached forgiveness in my ministry work, I couldn't very well rebuff another repentant sinner. Especially when I was married to her.

In 1991, I self-published a book called *Choosing and Loving Your Wife God's Way*. It was a self-help book for Christian couples on how to love each other in a godly manner. I should have taken my own advice. The second time I caught Lynette cheating was too much for me to stomach. I didn't actually catch her in the act, but I suspected something was up when she began getting strange phone calls and whispering into the receiver while I was in the other room. So I decided to stage my own little sting operation.

"The phone's been tapped and I've heard all your conversations," I told Lynette with a straight face, mustering all the acting skills I'd picked up on various movie sets over the years. "I want to know who you've been sleeping with."

Instead of an Oscar, I got the booby prize. Lynette told me who she had been sleeping with, how they met, and how long they had been carrying on their affair. After I heard the whole sordid tale, it was my turn to confess. I told her that I had tricked her and the phones weren't really tapped.

"Well, you dirty son of a bitch!" she said, throwing her shoe at me. No surprise there, but what came next was a stunner.

"I still want you back," Lynette told me. But this time I wasn't buying it. To be honest, my heavyweight ego was smarting. I had always done the cheating in the past; no woman had ever cheated on me before, and it was a bitter taste of my own medicine. It rattled me so much that I had a momentary lapse of reason and thought of hiring professionals to have Lynette and her lover killed. Can you imagine that? After all those years of preaching to convicted murderers in prisons all over the country, reminding them of God's law against killing, in a fit of emotion it went right out of my own head.

Once again, God intervened in my life when he put me in touch with an old friend. I got a phone call from Kenny Rainford, asking me to visit him in England and speak at a boxing dinner. I accepted in the blink of an eye, figuring the trip would clear my mind.

Rainford, a professional light heavyweight boxer in England, had been a fan of mine ever since he saw me fight Jimmy Ellis and Muhammad Ali on television in 1977. Rainford lived on the Wirral and did most of his training in nearby Liverpool. The boxing hero of most fight fans in England is Henry Cooper, but for Kenny Rainford, it was me.

Rainford started following my career as a nine-year-old kid. He loves to tell the story how he was sitting on the couch when the Ali-Shavers fight came on. Rainford watched the full 15 rounds, and then started collecting all the available video footage of my fights, even exhibition bouts. He probably knew more about me than I knew about myself. When he was old enough, he eventually trained in the United States to jump-start his own career as a light heavyweight.

Kenny trained in Louisiana under the tutelage of Beau Williford. He got my phone number through a mutual friend and asked me to help him out. It was the start of a long friendship.

I discovered I enjoyed training, giving advice, and sharing my ring knowledge with Kenny. In turn, Kenny was easy to teach and was willing to pay the price. He listened well, trained hard, and was dedicated to the sport. I even had him chopping trees. He reminded me a lot of myself during my climb to the top.

Kenny's first 11 fights were in the United States, but he had a security company he had started back home that was beginning to take off. He went back to England, but we stayed in touch. Now he wanted me over in jolly ol' England to train him and do some public relations for his security business. It sounded like a blast, and I took the lad up on his offer.

I flew over in early 1998 and had a great time. I made a few personal appearances for Kenny's company, Security Conscious, that went over very well. In England, boxers are revered to the point of worship. It felt good to be in the presence of true fans, and I enjoyed myself so much that when Kenny approached me with an idea he had, I didn't think twice before accepting.

"Earnie, business is very good since you've been here," he said. "I want you to move here so I can put you on a lifetime salary and benefits."

I told him I'd be back as soon as I tied up some loose ends in the States.

"Honey, I'm home," I said in a pleasant tone to Lynette as I walked through the door in Aurora. "But I'm leaving again just as soon as I get my bags packed."

When she found out what I had in mind, Lynette started right in with the honey-glazed Bible talk.

"Earnie, God said that we must forgive others or He won't forgive us," Lynette said. "Do you forgive me?"

"I do, Lynette," I answered.

But forgiveness was the least of what she wanted from me. Putting her hand on my arm, Lynette purred, "Darling, please fly me over to England with you so I can show you how much I love you. I want to be with you and only you."

"The only things I'm taking to England," I told her, "are these suitcases. I'm leaving all the excess baggage behind, including you."

She got the message loud and clear, followed by divorce papers shortly thereafter.

This Acorn was on a roll.

CHAPTER TWENTY

Henry the VIII, I Am

I arrived back in England on May 5, 1998, and made my home base on the Wirral. I grew up in a small town and I guess I've always been a small-town boy at heart. I was never one for the fast lane.

The pace in England is different than the pace in the United States. The country is beautiful, the people are friendly, and I also discovered the women are just as beautiful as they are in the States.

I was holding the heavy bag for Kenny one day when in walked his aunt, a beautiful lady named Sue Clegg. Kenny introduced us and we started a long conversation that we later continued over a cup of tea. It was so English, and very romantic. Two lumps or three, luv?

Even though she was 17 years younger than I was, Sue was very mature for her age. She was also a looker, which didn't hurt at all. After she left the gym, I threw an arm around Kenny and told him, "You can start calling me 'uncle.'"

But a man cannot live on love alone. More good news came in a phone call from a man named Tommy Miller. Miller was a speaking engagement agent who wanted to make both of us very rich. He reminded me of Don King, though, in that every angle he pitched seemed designed to make him just a little richer than me. Now that I was a full-time resident of Great Britain, Miller had it figured that under his management I could hit the after-dinner circuit running.

"I can get you 300 pounds ($500) a night and I'll keep you very busy," he said when we got together. All I had to do was sign.

"Let me think about it," I said. Three hundred pounds a night was pretty measly. I had always been paid more for my appearances in the States. I called my friend John Conteh, the ex-light heavyweight champion, who lived in England. Sure enough, Conteh said I should at least get paid a minimum of 1,500 pounds a night, or about $2,000. I called Miller back and told him my new asking price. Knowing a good thing when he saw it, he agreed and I signed on the dotted line.

But I didn't start right out in a bib and tucker. First I did some homework. Public speaking is one of the hardest things to do and especially do well. I always wanted to excel at everything I did, so after I signed the contract with Miller I went to the public library and read every book on public speaking I could get my hands on. I made notes, worked on my diction, practiced my speech in front of a mirror, and made sure to always speak in a clear, distinct voice.

Boxing isn't the only undertaking in which you need a good hook. In public speaking, the "hook" is something that grabs your audience right off the bat and keeps them hanging on your every word. My hook came after I told my listeners, "Good evening, ladies and gentleman, I want to thank you for being here, because you paid!" Then I'd tell them, "I am the only fighter in the world to ever beat Don King at his own game." That got 'em, and you could see everybody lean in for a closer listen as I told the story of how I tricked King in a court of law and how every contract has a loophole in it. Then I'd regale them with stories about the Mafia, and how I collected wives as fast as I knocked out opponents, and how it was I ended up tending to my neat bungalow garden in the quiet little town of Moreton on the Wirral.

I don't like to brag, but from beginning to end I had them in the palm of my hand. It was great fun. I am a natural ham, and now I was getting paid for it.

I learned to entertain my audience with spellbinding speeches. For speaking engagements I arrived early and usually stayed until the last customer left. I thanked everyone for showing up and shook every last hand to let the patrons know I appreciated them. This was something I picked up from Ali.

Word of mouth got me more engagements, and then Robert Yates of the tabloid newspaper *The Observer Life* in London called. He wanted to do a big feature story on me for the Sunday paper, which had the largest circulation for the week.

The British tabloids are much different than newspapers in the United States in that they rarely let the facts get in the way of a good story. That was fine by me. I figured I could even use their sensationalism to my own advantage. I had learned from Don King that a little negative publicity isn't necessarily a bad thing. Look at how singer/actress Madonna had masterfully manipulated the media for so many years, using bad publicity to keep her career going strong. Good news is nice to send home to Mom, but when the news is bad, everybody wants to read it.

I rolled out the red carpet for Yates. Figuring he would want to speak to some people back in the States who knew me, I gave him the phone numbers of Blackie Gennaro and La Verne, who I knew I could count on to burn up the transatlantic wire with a torrent of negative feedback on me.

Yates' article, titled "Life After Ali," appeared in *The Observer Life* on October 10, 1998. It began:

> He was the hardest puncher ever, owner of the fiercest right hand in boxing history. In the 1970s, he left Muhammad Ali shaken, pummeled Larry Holmes, but never won a title fight. Then a strange thing happened to Earnie Shavers. The big man from Alabama retired, of all things, to Wirral. Armed with tips from Bob Monkhouse, he braves the hostile crowds at social clubs as an after dinner speaker and evangelist. How the mighty have fallen.

Fallen, hell. After the article appeared I received an avalanche of requests from other reporters for interviews. That piece triggered a media sensation, and the phone didn't stop ringing for a year. I ended up doing 20-25 speaking engagements a month, and made extra peddling merchandise and autographs. I put Sue in charge of all of the money and we traveled all over England, Scotland, Wales, and Ireland. We had fun getting to know each other, acting like two school kids in love.

One of my most rewarding experiences in England was meeting Denzel Washington at a special preview of his movie

The Hurricane in London. The event was attended by several of England's former world boxing champions, including Nigel Benn, Chris Eubank, and John Conteh. At the party after the screening, Conteh introduced me to Washington, whose movies I had always enjoyed.

"Earnie Shavers!" Washington exclaimed as we shook hands. "I saw you fight Ali. Are you from England?" The whole room broke out in laughter.

Life overseas offered unique experiences and opportunities. When I wasn't on the road speaking, I became the official greeter at Yates' House in Queen Square in Liverpool.

"Come in and shake the hand that shook the world," I tell anyone within reach. I must say, I love greeting the customers. If trouble breaks out or someone gets too boozed up, I let the bouncers handle it. My mixing-it-up days are long past.

When people told me I was the friendliest doorman they had ever met, I politely corrected them by saying, "I am a greeter, and my job is to greet you if you get past the doorman."

It didn't take long before Sue and I began living together in a flat in Moreton. She gave up her job as a dental assistant so she could travel with me full-time.

My friends back home in the United States often asked if adjusting to a whole new culture was difficult. Not very, with one or two exceptions. The biggest adjustment was to the British automobile traffic, which as anyone who has ever seen a James Bond flick knows, runs opposite of that in the U.S. If you're an American, the British drive on the wrong side, or as Sue says, the "other side" of the road. More than one absent-minded Yankee has met his demise by looking to the left before crossing the street, only to get clobbered from the right. At some street crossings there are even signs posted warning pedestrians to look to the right before crossing.

I also learned that at speaking engagements, and especially formal gatherings, the host will occasionally say grace. Cheerio to that. After the main dinner course is finished, then the Loyal Toast to Her Majesty's health is always offered. After that people light up their smokes, but never before the toast.

Things picked up for me again across the pond after *Sports Illustrated* ran a piece on me called "Catching Up with Earnie

Shavers" in November 1999. I received a ton of letters from fans, friends, and family members saying they had seen the story, and the coverage of my thriving after-dinner speaking business eventually led to me signing with marketing agent Jerry Haack of Newport Marketing in Michigan. Haack got my fee up to $5,000 an appearance for card shows, autograph signings, Fight Nights, grand openings, speaking engagements, and corporate functions.

I was in demand on two continents. One of my trips back to the states brought me back to my old stomping grounds. On February 5, 2000, at the Packard Music Hall in Warren, Ohio, I received an award naming me "Puncher of the Century." It came from my old manager, Dean Chance, who reentered the World of boxing in the mid-80s. Ironically, Chance reunited with Blackie Gennaro to form a sanctioning body known as the International Boxing Council. But that oil-and-water combination still didn't work, and after they broke up again, Chance went on to found the International Boxing Association.

The award wasn't far-fetched. During my 88-bout professional career, I knocked out 68 of the 73 fighters I'd beaten, including two former heavyweight champions. That's one of the highest knockout percentages in the history of boxing.

In front of a packed house, Chance presented me with a specially inscribed clock before the main event of a card headlined by, of all people, Brian "B-52" Yates, the guy who'd clocked me himself in my last fight. But not even that could detract from the occasion for me, because all the friends and family who supported me over the years were in the crowd as Chance said, "There may have been better fighters, but I believe none had the pure punching power that Earnie did." The best thing about the award was I wouldn't have to give up the title until the next century, and my spot in history was guaranteed at least until then.

You can debate the merits of my career if you like, but there's no denying I was one lucky fighter. A lot of guys with more talent and fewer fights than I had ended up in pretty sad shape. I took a few beatings—my second match with Larry Holmes and the war with Tex Cobb come to mind—but by and large the Acorn came out uncracked. Look at some of the guys

I fought. Muhammad Ali's slurred speech and other physical ailments have been well documented. He was diagnosed with Parkinson's disease. I'm not a doctor, but I know a few of the beatings he took in his later years, along with the punishment received in too many grueling sparring sessions, had to have contributed to his demise in 2016.

And is there a sadder story than that of Jerry Quarry? He died in 1999. Quarry was a crowd-pleaser who fought them all, but the punches he took exacted a horrible toll. Near the end of his life he needed help feeding himself and changing clothes. He'd wander the streets in Hemet, California, oblivious to his surroundings, and the police would pick him up and take him home. Doctors said he had the brain of an 80-year-old when he was only 50. What that brave Irishman went through at the end of his life was horrible for Jerry, his family, friends, and fans.

Probably more boxers than we are aware of suffer from "dementia pugilistica"—the medical term for punch drunk. You only hear about some of the big-name boxers who exhibit the symptoms, but there are countless other ex-boxers who suffer the same fate after taking too many shots to the head. After a few decades of this, the limbic system, which controls an individual's memory, is destroyed. Many boxers go undiagnosed because they don't ever get tested, and some, like Quarry, who showed signs of brain impairment in a 1983 test, fight on because boxing is what they know best. Brain trauma is the downside of a sport that also gives hope and opportunity to countless others.

I thank God every day to have come through my boxing career in good shape. I also give thanks for never causing an opponent's death or serious injury. It's pretty well documented that most head traumas in boxing are caused by an accumulation of punches. I usually got the job done with just one or two.

I'm often asked to name the fighters I think left an indelible mark on the sport with special skills. I always say that my good friend Larry Holmes had the best jab I ever saw. He dominated the heavyweight division for seven years behind that spear-like jab. It was like a surgical tool, and I should know—I was on the receiving end of it for 23 rounds. It landed within the blink of an eye, kept fighters at bay, and did major damage at the same time.

The best right hand was owned by Joe Louis. Once the "Brown Bomber" found his range with it, the issue was usually settled and the other guy went bye-bye.

The best left hook belonged hands down to "Smokin'" Joe Frazier. I'm glad not to be speaking from personal experience in this case. Frazier could throw that looping left to the head or the body with equally damaging results. Who'll ever forget the sight of Ali flying on his back from it in his first go with Joe?

The best uppercut? For all of Mike Tyson's wasted talent and ability, no fighter at any weight ever did more damage punching up. "Iron Mike" turned his diminutiveness to his advantage by mastering the art of the uppercut. Ask Marvis Frazier, Joe's son, who was almost decapitated by one in their fight. Tyson's left uppercut was just as deadly as his right.

The best in-fighter was Jack Dempsey. They didn't call him the "Manassa Mauler" for nothing. This legendary champion of the 1920s was a whirlwind puncher who struck savagely at every open part of his opponent's body. Ever see a film of Dempsey's title-winning match against Jess Williard? Just make sure you don't watch it after a heavy meal. Dempsey's short punches rearranged facial features and took the fight out of anyone who traded with him.

The best stamina I attribute to John "The Boston Strong Boy" Sullivan, the last and best of the bare-knuckled bullies. Boxers of Sullivan's era commonly ran 10 to 20 miles of roadwork every day in training. Sullivan dined on beef or mutton chops three times a day to maintain his constitution. If you doubt my words, try lugging Jake Kilrain around for 75 rounds in the sweltering Mississippi summer heat, as Sullivan did in 1889.

Best ring generalship goes to Jersey Joe Walcott. When it came to executing a game plan, Walcott was like an Army tactician. He used every inch of available ring space to his advantage, maneuvering his opponents into position for his assaults, and then dancing away when they returned fire. Walcott was without equal, and students of the fight game study his slick moves to this day. His ring smarts made good fighters look like beginners and great ones look average.

The biggest heart belonged to Primo "The Ambling Alp" Carnera. A lot of fight experts characterize the Italian giant as nothing more than a "sham champion" and a blight on the sport, but who was gamer in the ring? Consider this: Carnera was dropped 11 times by Max Baer, but got up every time, and was still standing when the ref stopped the fight. He never once gave hint of a yellow streak, despite taking some of the worst beatings in heavyweight history.

The toughest and best body puncher was Rocky "The Brockton Blockbuster" Marciano. To Marciano, anything above the waist was fair game. He brutally hammered his foe's arms, shoulders, and sides until they were battered and bruised and they couldn't raise their gloves anymore, and then shifted his attack upstairs. You came out of a fight with Rocky Marciano looking like you'd been through a meat grinder. And tough? The famous photo of the "Rock" pulling apart his nose after Ezzard Charles literally split it down the middle speaks volumes about the undefeated champion's toughness.

And on the eighth day, God created Ali.

The best chin, footwork, defense, and hand speed belonged to the "Athlete of the 20th Century," Muhammad Ali.

Think about it. He conquered eight world heavyweight champions: Patterson, Liston, Ellis, Terrell, Frazier, Norton, Foreman, and Spinks. He also faced fearsome competitors like Cleveland Williams, Zora Folley, Ron Lyle, Jerry Quarry, George Chuvalo, and myself, and none of us could bring him down. We damned sure tried, but the man had a chin that belongs on Mount Rushmore.

"Float like a butterfly" was his mantra, but before Ali sat out three years as a conscientious objector of the Vietnam war, his feet hardly seemed to touch the canvas. He was like a ninja warrior walking across rice paper without leaving a footprint. Welterweights have struggled to master the footwork Ali perfected as a heavyweight. He was truly a sight to behold.

Ali's great reflexes allowed him to evade punches and escape without a scratch against the likes of Liston, Williams, and me. Later in his career, after time slowed him down a bit, he perfected the "rope-a-dope" and evaded blows even when laying on the ropes.

At his best, Ali dazzled with combinations that confounded his challengers, even when the punches were mere taps. His hands were blurs when the combinations began to flow, and he could counter a punch even before it got within landing distance.

One of the proudest possessions I own is a letter from Ali thanking me for attending his 50th birthday party in 1992:

> Dear Earnie:
>
> My wife Lonnie and I would like to personally thank you for taking time out of your busy schedule to help celebrate and entertain at my 50th Birthday Celebration at the Wiltern Theatre. Your presence helped to make this affair one of "the Greatest" events of my life. I realize that it was a sacrifice for someone like you who is as "great" as I am....
>
> You have been one of my favorites throughout the years, and I am truly grateful and honored that you were able to appear before my family, friends, and peers for this celebration.
>
> We pray for your continued success and may all your endeavors prove to be rewarding. May God bless you.
>
> Sincerely,
>
> Muhammad Ali

As for me, I'd be more than happy going to my grave being considered the hardest puncher of all time. In fact, I already have my plot chosen and know what the stone over me will read:

> Here lies a man who plied his trade in the toughest division of a brutal sport, a true gentleman in possession of the nastiest punch God ever created.

You know, the 1970s are widely considered to have been the Golden Era of Heavyweights because so many good fighters were competing then. There were Muhammad Ali, Joe Frazier, Larry Holmes, George Foreman, Ken Norton, Ron Lyle, Jerry Quarry, Jimmy Ellis, Oscar Bonavena, George Chuvalo, Jimmy Ellis, and myself. I nominate Holmes as the most underrated of the bunch. That's because he came up right behind Ali, whose charisma bathed Larry in a lesser light. I already talked about the Holmes jab, but his chin was something else, too. I'm still wondering how he got up from that right hand I laid on him.

It wasn't just our talent that puts us over today's crop of heavyweights. We were more disciplined and took better care of ourselves.

I did everything I could to get an advantage over my competition. I'd go to bed earlier and wake up sooner. I'd refrain from sex and alcohol. Heck, I'd even eat more raw eggs than the rest. I'm not sure how many of today's heavyweights are willing to pay the price to be the best.

Not only did we have great talent in the 1970s, but we also had world-class trainers to impart their wisdom to the fighters. Guys like Eddie Futch, Angelo Dundee, Emanuel Steward, Ray Arcel, Bill Slayton, Willie Ketchum, Cus D'Amato and Freddie Brown. They prepared us perfectly to fight.

Today's boxers may be much wealthier in a strictly material sense than we ever dreamed of being, but I believe all of my experiences and contacts throughout the years have immeasurably enriched me as a human being.

Do I have regrets? Sure, a lot of them. Every time I got knocked out or lost in the ring, I deeply regretted it. Mainly I regret not going for the jugular when I had Ali on the ropes in the second round of our championship fight.

Outside the ring, my main regret is messing around with another women while I was married to La Verne. It led to our break up, and ultimately the break up of my family. My infidelity caused me and people I loved many heartaches, and things would be different if I had a chance to do it all over again.

All in all, the fight game has been one of the greatest blessings that God could have given to me and my family. I'll never badmouth the sport because it continues to open doors for me.

CHAPTER TWENTY-ONE

Roll the Dice

I would have been perfectly content living out my golden years with Sue Clegg in our comfortable bungalow in The Wirral, in northwest England, had it not been for a late-night phone call from one of my daughters in the States.

After all, I had a nice-paying job making appearances on behalf of Kenny Rainford's security company, and all the speaking engagements I wanted; plus, after having vacuumed up so much money from my fight purses over the years, Uncle Sam had finally started doling some of it back to me in the form of monthly Social Security checks. It wasn't a lot, but it was regular.

What's more, if I say so myself, I was a beloved figure in the United Kingdom, a place with a hallowed pugilistic tradition and known for its admiration of boxers. Except for the food (only a native Brit would consider "kippers"—cold-smoked herring—a proper breakfast) and a little wet weather, England was a perfectly fine place to live and this son of a sharecropper counted himself abundantly blessed to have found a home in a place he never dreamed he would live out his days. (I wasn't the only one surprised about that. One English sportswriter wrote, "The Wirral is where former Liverpool and Everton players run mock Tudor pubs. Running into Earnie Shavers there is like finding Ian Callaghan or Bob Latchford living in Buffalo Crotch, Arkansas.")

At age 67, I was happy and comfortable, and didn't think anything could ever make me pull up stakes again.

Four words from my daughter Tamara changed that in a heartbeat when she phoned that night: "Daddy, I miss you."

I had been in England for almost a dozen years, and while everything else had fallen nicely into place the one thing I could never get acclimated to was seeing my kids intermittently.

During my occasional visits to the States I'd see them as much as possible, but saying goodbye to them again never got any easier. My nine babies were now all grown up, had good-paying jobs, kids of their own, and were doing very well. Well and good—but they were still and always would be my babies. And happy as I was with my life across the Big Pond, missing them was a hurt that never went away.

Tamara's plaintive words hit me harder than any punch ever had, and as soon as I hung up the phone I knew it was time to go back home. Not just for an extended visit, either. I needed to go back to the States for good.

As quick as that decision was made, the whole rest of the night I spent grappling with the next one: how would I break the news to Sue? She had been my companion for the last decade. Sue was easy-going, kind, polite, and never made any waves, and I figured when it came right down to it she would readily pack her bags and go to America with me.

But Sue's British roots run deep; her entire family lived in the area. "Auntie Sue" was a bedrock of the Rainsford clan and could be counted on as a shoulder to lean on, a voice of reason, and someone to dispense reasonable, reliable advice in a crisis.

There was also the fact that we were not man and wife, though marriage had been discussed from time to time. Sue was a widow and more than once had pointedly referred to her late husband as "the love of my life," a pretty definitive declaration of where we stood. I never cajoled or argued about it, and she showed me the same consideration when I told her I was leaving for good in one week. In fact, our parting was almost comically easy. A week later when I stood at the door with two suitcases and turned to say farewell, Sue just said, "Okay, I'll see you," and gave me a kiss on the cheek.

Pip pip, cheerio, and all that rot.

My plan was to move back to Phoenix, Arizona, where I lived prior to moving to England. I liked Phoenix for its incessant sunshine, affordable cost of living, and because of my knowledge of their church culture. The city had a small black population and its church system was like one big family. While I had remained faithful to the word of God in England, finding a church to share fellowship took some doing. England is notoriously agnostic and residents who identify themselves as non-believers far outnumber the other kind. Now I needed to immerse myself again in a strong Christian culture.

I couldn't catch a direct flight to Phoenix and had a layover in Las Vegas. At the airport I grabbed a bite to eat and checked my phone for voice messages. The most intriguing one was from a man named Bill Watson, who operated a business called Memorabilia International at Planet Hollywood Resort on the Vegas Strip. Today Bill represents hundreds of current and former professional athletes and is one of the true moguls in the sports autograph/memorabilia industry.

When I called him back, Bill told me about his business and made an earnest pitch (my favorite kind) to represent me. He said if I was interested he could guarantee me full-time work at autograph shows in Vegas, around the country, and abroad.

Adios, Phoenix. After I checked into a nearby hotel I called a real estate agent. It was a roll of the dice, but Vegas was where I would be hanging my gloves for a while. The Lord does indeed work in mysterious ways.

There are more high rollers than Holy Rollers in Sin City, but the Good Lord steered me there for a reason. More than one, actually. Among the first events Bill set up for me was an appearance at a sports store inside McCarran International Airport. During a break from signing photos and boxing gloves for fans, a stunning looking black lady dressed to the nines approached the table and asked, "Are you Mike...?"

I knew right away who she meant. "Oh, no," I said with a big smile, "Mike Tyson would be my little brother." Then I introduced myself and explained that Mike and I belonged to the rare brotherhood of heavyweight boxers. Her name was Rita Williams, and for the next few minutes we chatted pleasantly. When she said good-bye and turned to walk away, a distinct inner voice told me: "She's going to be your wife."

About an hour later I got up to stretch my legs and took a walk. A couple doors down was Marshall Rousso, a high-end fashion store for women, and as I idly glanced in the window who should I spy but the beauteous Rita Williams, dressing a mannequin. Turns out she managed the store.

I tapped on the window, and when she looked over I smiled and proclaimed, "Miss, I'm gonna marry you." Then I headed back to the autograph session. Later Rita told me that she was shocked, but not so much that she didn't take the opportunity to check out my backside and think, *I like that man's stride!*

We never had what you'd call a conventional date. Both of us were busy in our careers. Rita managed two stores and routinely pulled double shifts, while I made many personal appearances and signings each month, and travelled often. But that didn't stop me from letting her know from the get-go that I wanted us to be married as soon as possible.

"Let me think about it," Rita said. Like me, she was a devoted Christian, so I urged her to pray about it. I understood her wariness. She'd heard about professional athletes—boxers in particular—who racked up conquests in the bedroom as enthusiastically as they did in the ring. Plus, Rita was twice divorced, and the mother of a son and daughter. We talked often on the phone, candidly exchanging information about our pasts and the hard lessons we had learned, and sharing our mutual conviction that God had something better in store for us. Each conversation drew us closer.

Still, it took two years, lots of prayer, and three ardent marriage proposals from me for Rita to finally come around. We were married on August 31, 2014, in one of those neon wedding chapels off the Vegas Strip. I thought having that Marshall Rousso mannequin as maid of honor would be a nice touch, but that didn't fly with Rita.

Rita became my full-fledged partner, even becoming co-manager of my career. In preparation for that I gave her a quick course in Boxing 101 predicated on a fundamental truth I learned the hard way during all my years in the sport.

"*Everybody* in the fight game is shady," I told her, emphasizing the first word. "If your own mother is involved in it, don't believe a word she says. No one in boxing tells the truth."

Rita aced the course. She was a quick study and used the impeccable organizational skills from her successful career as a manager for the Marshall Retail Group to kick my career into high gear. She established a baseline price for my personal appearances and autograph sessions, inserted stipulations in my business contracts that guaranteed me per diem payments and other perks, and always kept an eagle-eye out for my protection and best interests. If I'd had Rita back when I was dealing with Don King, he wouldn't have been known for that trademark electric hairdo because he'd have torn it all out by the roots.

Rita's intuition is uncanny. She has a sense when someone isn't trustworthy. She'll tell me, "Don't fool with that person." She has never made a bad call.

My work enabled the two of us to travel across America and to foreign countries. Best of all, we were able to see and spend time with old friends like Larry Holmes, one of the pillars of the 1970s era of great heavyweights. We competed against one another in some of the most hotly contested fights in ring history, and to date our admiration and mutual friendship has remained. My travels throughout the years enabled me to keep in touch with so many great fighters of my era such as Muhammad Ali, Joe Frazier, Ken Norton and George Foreman.

While we threw many blows in the ring, the worst ones to take were outside the ring as these boxing champions began fading in the sunset. Joe Frazier went first in 2011, followed two years later by Ken Norton. Then the biggest blow of all—Ali in 2016.

I usually saw Ali a couple of times a year and it was always fantastic to just be around The Champ. He was always so playful and loved pulling stunts on all of us (one of his favorites was snapping his fingers in my ear when I wasn't looking). But for all the pains he took to hide and minimize it, he suffered mightily from the ravages of Parkinson's disease, the progressive neurological condition that eventually robbed him of his unique voice and equally singular physical dexterity.

He had opened so many doors for me since we met in 1973, and those favors never stopped. Anytime I needed something from him, Ali was there for me and never asked for or expected anything in return.

Was there another athlete who transcended his sport more than this great man? No. Ali unified the races, religions, young and old. He was a selfless humanitarian, a statesman, a lode star, an idol worthy of the name. This acorn is immensely proud to have known, fought, and embraced the mightiest oak of them all. We shared a mutual love and admiration for each other.

The last time I saw Ali was in Vegas, and my heart told me it was likely our final meeting. On June 4, 2016, my phone started to blow up with voice mails and texts. Ali had died at the Phoenix-area hospital where he was being treated for respiratory complications. He was 74.

As supernaturally gifted as Ali was as a boxer, you don't spend almost 30 years in the ring (he started at age 12) without paying a heavy price for that honor. Jonathan Eig, author of *Ali: A Life*, estimated the number of punches Ali took at about 200,000—266 of those came from me in our one and only bout. The latest research shows that every single blow to the head, whether in boxing, football, or just bouncing a soccer ball off your noggin', affects the brain. For obvious reasons, I'd just as soon think about almost anything else. But we all knew and accepted the risks of participating in a blood sport, and if the time should ever come for me to pay the piper, I hope and pray I'll do it with the same grace and courage as my dear friend.

Now that I'm in my seventies, I look at things in accordance with the old axiom that every day above ground is a good day. Youth is fun and exciting, but there are rewards to growing older and wiser. The first time around was great, but I wouldn't trade what I've got now for another ride on that merry-go-round. My greatest hope is that Rita and my children and grandchildren will enjoy the fruits of my labor and live happy lives.

By the way, proceeds from this book will go to nine under-privileged children and one old lady. Did I mention I have nine underprivileged children and one old lady? (Badum-CHING!)

They say good things come to those who wait, and I say "Hallelujah!" to that. The Bible tells us our eyes cannot behold what God has planned for us. That is what He spoke to me when I became a Christian in 1986. He was just waiting for me to get my life in order. Now that it is and I have the glorious peace of mind that comes with God's saving grace, I'm ready for the "Big Time" once again.

Earnie Shavers' Fight Record

1969

Nov 6	Red Howell	Las Vegas, NV	KO 2
Nov 11	George Holden	Orlando, FL	KO 1
Nov 14	Stanley Johnson	Seattle, WA	L 6
Nov 21	Lee Roy	Rapid City, SD	KO 3
Dec 4	J.D. McCauley	Akron, OH	KO 2
Dec 18	Chico Froncano	Canton, OH	KO 1
Dec 26	Gene Idilette	Orlando, FL	KO 2

1970

Jan 7	Tiger Brown	Akron, OH	KO 1
Jan 24	Joe Byrd	Canton, OH	KO 3
Jan 27	Tiger Brown	Orlando, FL	KO 5
Mar 6	Arthur Miller	Canton, OH	KO 1
Mar 23	Ray Asher	Youngstown, OH	KO 1
Apr 14	Frank Smith	Canton, OH	KO 4
May 11	Ron Stander	Omaha, NE	KO by 5
Aug 29	Jim Daniels	Youngstown, OH	KO 1
Sep 12	Don Branch	Columbus, OH	KO 1
Oct 14	Johnny Hudgins	Canton, OH	KO 1
Nov 18	Johnny Mac	Youngstown, OH	KO 4
Dec 7	Bunky Akins	New York, NY	KO 1

1971

Jan 6	Lee Estes	Akron, OH	KO 2
Jan 15	Nat Shaver	Miami Beach, FL	KO 1
Feb 3	Johnny Mac	Las Vegas, NV	KO 3
Feb 17	Richard Gosha	Akron, OH	KO 5
Mar 3	Steve Carter	Las Vegas, NV	KO 1
Mar 24	Young Agabab	Las Vegas, NV	KO 1
Apr 21	Mac Harrison	Akron, OH	KO 2
Apr 24	Willie Johnson	Tampa, FL	KO 4
May 14	Jimmy Brown	Las Vegas, NV	KO 1
Jun 1	Chuck Leslie	Stateline, NY	KO 10
Jun 30	Bill Hardney	Warren, OH	KO 1
Jul 13	Bill McMurray	Stateline, NY	KO 1
Sep 28	Pat Duncan	Reno, NV	KO 5
Oct 17	Charlie Boston	Akron, OH	KO 2
Oct 29	Elmo Henderson	Stateline, NY	KO 4
Nov 23	Cleo Daniels	Warren, OH	KO 2
Nov 30	Del Morris	Bryant, IN	KO 3

1972

Feb 1	Ted Gullick	Warren, OH	KO 6
Feb 15	Elgie Waters	Beaumont, TX	KO 2
Apr 6	Charlie Polite	Warren, OH	KO 3
Apr 22	Bob Felstein	Akron, OH	KO 5
May 5	Lou Bailey	Akron, OH	KO 2
Aug 26	Vicente Rondon	Canton, OH	KO 10
Sep 22	A.J. Staples	Canton, OH	KO 1
Oct 25	Leroy Caldwell	Newton Falls, OH	KO 2

1973

Feb 19	Jimmy Young	Philadelphia, PA	KO 1
May 12	Harold Carter	Windsor, Ontario	KO 1
Jun 18	Jimmy Ellis	New York, NY	KO 1
Dec 14	Jerry Quarry	New York, NY	KO by 1

1974

May 16	Cookie Wallace	San Jose, CA	KO 1
Nov 4	Bob Stallings	New York, NY	L 10
Nov 26	Jimmy Young	Landover, MD	D 10

1975

Feb 11	Leon Shaw	Orlando, FL	KO 1
Apr 9	Rochelle Norris	Binghamton, NY	KO 10
May 8	Oliver Wright	Baltimore, MD	TKO 3
Sep 13	Ron Lyle	Denver, CO	KO by 6
Nov 13	Tommy Howard	Monroeville, PA	KO 3

1976

Mar 28	Henry Clark	Paris, France	W 10
Sep 28	Henry Clark	Bronx, NY	TKO 2
Dec 11	Roy Williams	Las Vegas, NV	TKO 10

1977

Apr 16	Howard Smith	Las Vegas, NY	TKO 2
Sep 29	Muhammad Ali	New York, NY	L15
	for World Heavyweight Title		

1978

Mar 25	Larry Holmes	Las Vegas, NV	L 12
	WBC Title Eliminator		
Jul 20	Harry Terrell	Virginia Beach, VA	KO 2
Oct 9	John Girowski	Hampton, VA	KO 4
Dec 4	Harold Carter	Saginaw, MI	KO 3

1979

Mar 23	Ken Norton	Las Vegas, NV	TKO 1
May 25	Eddie Porette	Richfield, OH	KO 3
Sep 28	Larry Holmes	Las Vegas, NV	TKO by 11
	for WBC Heavyweight Title		

1980

Mar 8	Bernardo Mercado	Great Gorge, KY	KO by 7
Jun 14	Leroy Boone	Cincinnati, OH	W 10
Aug 2	Randall "Tex" Cobb	Detroit, MI	TKO by 8
Oct 17	Ted Hamilton	West Palm Beach, FL	KO 2

1981

Jul 29	Terrel Williams	Saginaw, MI	KO 2
Sep 9	Mike Rodger	Lansing, MI	KO 2
Dec 11	Jeff Sims	Nassau, Bahamas	KO 5

1982

Apr 21	Ali Haakim	Traverse City, MI	W 10
May 8	Joe Bugner	Dallas, TX	KO 2
May 15	Danny Sutton	Charleston, WV	KO 7
Jun 11	James Tillis	Las Vegas, NV	L 10
Jun 22	Billy Joe Thomas	Houston, TX	KO 5
Aug 17	Walter Santemore	Lafayette, LA	L 10
Sep 5	Chuck Gardner	Wales, WI	KO 2
Oct 14	Phil Clinard	Tulsa, OK	KO 2
Nov 5	Tony Perea	El Paso, TX	KO 7

1983

| Jan 29 | Robin Griffin | El Paso, TX | W 10 |
| Mar 1 | George Chaplin | Baltimore, MD | LDQ 9 |

1984–86 *(Inactive)*

1987

| May 16 | Larry Sims | Cincinnati, OH | KO 1 |

1988–94 *(Inactive)*

1995

| Sep 19 | Brian Morgan | Omaha, NE | W 8 |
| Nov 24 | Brian Yates | Baraboo, WI | TKO by 2 |

Acknowledgments

Thanks to Pete Ehrmann for his many hours of devotion in editing the first edition of this book. We must also thank Greg Korn for his eye for detail and getting the facts right. To Carolyn and Mike Terrill for their hours of editing. We appreciate the many efforts of people who helped in this project. They include: Jimmy Adams, Ben Gardner, Jerry Haack, Judy Haack, Bob Lynch, Kenny Rainford, Mike Siefert, and Bert Randolph Sugar.

And as usual, a big thank you to my wife, Zoe Terrill, who sacrificed her time so that I could indulge in my passion.

Marshall Terrill

．．．

MARSHALL TERRILL's work has been featured in many boxing publications, such as *The Ring*, *KO*, *The USA Boxing News*, and *International Boxing Digest*. He is the author of the best-selling biography, *Steve McQueen: Portrait of an American Rebel*, as well as co-author of *Ken Norton: Going the Distance*.